EDITOR NOTE There is an interesting history behind *Old No. 1*, Guy Clark's debut album. I wrote about it in *Without Getting Killed or Caught*, my 2016 biography of Guy. But it's difficult to include all the details of a single project in a biography that covers the entire arc of a life. As the 50th anniversary of *Old No. 1* approached, we (the folks at Guy Clark, LLC) thought it appropriate to dig a little deeper into the origins of this significant work and to celebrate it. Fifty years on, music lovers are still discovering Guy's body of work, starting with this first extraordinary collection of songs. We asked Natalie Weiner to sift through the credits and interview anyone and everyone who was there for the making of the album. Then we asked our friend Peter Blackstock, journalist and co-founder of *No Depression* magazine, to take Natalie's interviews, do his own research, and use his creative instincts and writing chops to pull together the history of *Old No. 1* and write this book. Of course, Peter nailed it. Big thanks to Natalie and Peter for their collective tender loving care on *Old No. 1 at 50*. Happy reading.

Tamara Saviano
Guy Clark, LLC

Old No. 1 at 50: A History of Guy Clark's First Album
Peter Blackstock

With interviews by Natalie Weiner
Edited by Tamara Saviano
Designed by Wendy Stamberger

Copyright © 2025 by Guy Clark LLC, Nashville, Tennessee

First Edition

ISBN: 979-8-218-79807-9

A HISTORY OF GUY CLARK'S FIRST ALBUM

BY PETER BLACKSTOCK

PUBLISHED BY GUY CLARK LLC

TABLE OF CONTENTS

INTRODUCTION

In her 2016 Guy Clark biography *Without Getting Killed or Caught*, author Tamara Saviano — without whom, to be clear, this book you're holding would not exist — recounts her own introduction to Guy's music. Listening to records with her father and a family friend at her home in Wisconsin, she heard *Old No. 1* for the first time, shortly after its release in November 1975. She was captivated from the start. "It was the beginning of my love affair with songwriters," Saviano wrote. "I bought my own copy of *Old No. 1* before the week was out."

As the author of this book, which focuses specifically on *Old No. 1* in honor of the album's 50th anniversary, I can only wish I had a first-encounter story as poetic as Tamara's 1975 epiphany. It would be another decade or so before I first heard *Old No. 1*, as an aspiring music journalist in mid-1980s Austin. Yet as a preteen in the early-mid '70s, I was already familiar with several of the album's songs. My oldest brother Silas was big fan of Jerry Jeff Walker back then, and the music drifting down the hallway from his room included Jerry Jeff's albums *Viva Terlingua* (1973) and *Ridin' High* (1975). The former included Guy's "Desperados Waiting for a Train," and "Coat From the Cold" was on the latter. "Being young and not very discerning, I was more taken with the performer than the composer," Si wrote to me recently when I asked him about Guy. "Now, I would feel differently."

Si didn't own Jerry Jeff's 1972 self-titled album, which included Guy's songs "L.A. Freeway" and "That Old Time Feeling." The former was a minor hit nationally but a major one in Austin, where I grew up. Local radio stations played it constantly, championing their local rising star. It's one of the songs I remember most vividly from my youth. Decades later, when I played *Old No. 1* for the woman I would marry, I took it as a very good sign that she loved "L.A. Freeway" instantly; in my mind's eye, I can still hear her singing along to the song at the first home we shared together in North Carolina.

By that time I was well into a 13-year run as co-editor and co-publisher of the Americana music magazine *No Depression*. (We featured Guy on the cover of our September-October 2002 issue.) Eventually I ended up back in Texas at the *Austin American-Statesman*, where I wrote an obituary for Guy after his death in May 2016. By then, I'd seen Guy perform around 20 times, starting with a solo show at Austin's Cactus Cafe in 1989, followed by many shows in Seattle in the 1990s and North Carolina in the 2000s, and finally a performance at Nashville's Belcourt Theater in 2009 while Guy was recovering from cancer.

When my wife Lisa and I moved to San Diego in 2023, it hadn't occurred to me that our new home city had a subtle but important connection to *Old No. 1*. Rereading Saviano's book as I prepared to write this one, I came across her account of a fateful night circa 1971 when Guy and his soon-to-be-wife Susanna had driven south from their home in Long Beach for a show Guy was playing at the Heritage Coffeehouse in San Diego. It was on the way home that Guy muttered the soon-to-be-immortal words, "If I could just get off of this L.A. freeway without getting killed or caught." So now, whenever we head north on I-5 toward Los Angeles, I imagine looking across the lanes of traffic, back through decades of time, to witness the moment that sparked one of the songs which made *Old No. 1* a masterpiece.

I envision this book as a companion to *Without Getting Killed or Caught,* and specifically a sort of expansion on her book's pivotal seventh chapter, which covered Guy's initial record deal with RCA that produced both *Old No. 1* and *Texas Cookin'*. While

I did the writing, I benefited greatly from the research Saviano did for her definitive 2016 Clark biography. Tamara shared with me more than a hundred interviews she'd conducted from 2000 to 2015, plus other interviews and press clippings she'd gathered. Equally vital were more than a dozen interviews done last fall and winter by Dallas country music journalist Natalie Weiner with key figures in the *Old No. 1* story, including most of the still-living musicians who took part in the sessions.

I supplemented that mountain of research with a few interviews of my own conducted over spring and summer 2025, plus interviews and articles from my archives. Along the way, some friends and acquaintances helped nail down hard-to-find details, including Nick West, Barry Mazor, Dave Thomas, David Menconi, Joe Nick Patoski, and two members of the Saviano-moderated "Without Getting Killed or Caught" Facebook group, Patrick Grogan and Criss Emmert. In addition, both Saviano and Rodney Crowell made themselves available to answer questions as I was writing. Thanks are also due to people who told me stories about *Old No. 1* that didn't make it into the book, including Bruce Lyon and Greg Ellis; and to Hector Saldana of the Wittliff Collections at Texas State University.

I'll give the final word of this beginning to Jerry Kroon, one of the drummers on *Old No. 1*, who offers further insight into the making of the album in Chapter Four. But this particular quote from him sums up the end result of the recording sessions, and the resulting album: "It seemed to work out really well. Evidently, it was a success, because they're celebrating it 50 years later. Not everybody can say that."

Peter Blackstock

CHAPTER ONE
THE LONG ROAD TO THE BEGINNING

Old No. 1 came out on RCA Records in November 1975, just as Guy Clark was turning 34 years old. It seems fair to say he was a late bloomer as a recording artist, given that many of the legendary Texas songwriters to whom Clark is often compared got an earlier start. Townes Van Zandt was two years younger than Guy; yet by the time *Old No. 1* came out, Townes had already released six albums. Similar story for Jerry Jeff Walker, whose 1972 cover of "L.A. Freeway" helped put Guy on the map nationally. By 1975, Walker, five months younger than Guy, had issued several solo albums plus band records in New York with Circus Maximus. Mickey Newbury, a mentor to both Guy and Townes, was just a year older than Guy but had five albums out by 1975. And Doug Sahm, who shares Guy's exact birthdate — November 6, 1941 — released three albums under his own name in 1973-74 after he'd had hit singles in the mid-1960s fronting the Sir Douglas Quintet.

Beyond Texas, renowned songwriters tended to be even younger when they began their recording careers. Bob Dylan was born the same year as Guy but already had a catalog beyond a dozen albums when *Old No. 1* surfaced. John Prine turned 25 in October 1971, the same month his now-iconic self-titled debut came out on Atlantic. Jackson Browne was 24 when Asylum issued his self-titled debut in January 1972. And Tom Waits also was 24 when Asylum released *Closing Time* in March 1973.

One big exception is illuminative: Kris Kristofferson. Born in 1936, he was five years older than Guy. But just like Guy, Kris turned 34 the same month that his debut album arrived in June

1970, titled simply *Kristofferson*. As such, it seems fitting that many reviews of *Old No. 1* in the national music press compared Clark's songwriting to Kristofferson's. While the two had very different upbringings, one reason neither of them had records on the shelves until their 30s was because they spent their 20s pursuing a variety of different avenues that helped define who they became as artists.

Kristofferson's early years were marked by a variety of experiences that clearly broadened his horizons. An Air Force brat, he graduated high school in the Bay Area before getting a bachelor's degree at Pomona College in Southern California and then, famously, moving on to England for a Rhodes Scholarship at the University of Oxford. He joined the Army in the early 1960s, living for a time with his wife and young daughter in West Germany. While there, he began playing music at bars on the Army base. After visiting Nashville while he was in the military, he gave up a career teaching at West Point to relocate to Music City in 1965 with a goal of pursuing music.

A janitorial job at Columbia Records gave him an early glimpse into the industry and recording studios, while a more adventurous gig as a helicopter pilot for Gulf of Mexico oil rigs helped set up what became one of his life's best-known details: He landed a helicopter on Johnny Cash's property to let Cash know how serious he was about becoming a songwriter. Cash got him on the bill for the 1969 Newport Folk Festival; less than a year later, *Kristofferson* arrived on Monument Records, loaded with original tunes that would become his calling-cards for the rest of his life — including "Me and Bobby McGee," "Help Me Make It Through the Night," "For the Good Times" and "Sunday Morning Coming Down."

Guy's experiences growing up and as a young adult were different but no less character-defining, and they certainly played a significant part in shaping many of the songs that ended up on

Old No. 1. Born in the small west Texas town of Monahans, Guy drew inspiration from characters such as oil wildcatter Jack Prigg, a close family friend who became the subject of "Desperados Waiting for a Train." Another man named Jack, the father of Guy's childhood pal Jerry Kittrell, worked at the Monahans train depot. He gets namechecked (along with old man Wileman, a local dominoes and checkers master) in "Texas 1947," which Guy wrote about being at the depot in the summer of 1947 as the whole town awaited the arrival of a red-and-silver streamline train.

The family's move to the Texas coastal town of Rockport during Guy's pre-teen years brought new characters who'd turn up in other songs, such as his high school English teacher Martha Ballou, whose surname he chose for *Old No. 1*'s opening track, "Rita Ballou." Guy's high school job working on boats at Rob Roy Rice's shipyard may not have directly informed *Old No. 1*, but it would show up in later songs such as "Boats To Build." And though Lola Bonner, a partner in his father Ellis Clark's law practice, didn't get namechecked in a song, she gave Guy guitar lessons that informed the sounds on *Old No. 1* and throughout Guy's career. (She also took him to see a performance by the legendary Spanish guitarist Andrés Segovia that Guy later said was "the highlight of my life.")

Guy's coming-of-age years in Houston in the 1960s brought a bounty of new experiences that helped shape the lens through which he viewed the world, and thus inevitably how he wrote his songs as well. In 1963, he underwent Peace Corps training in Puerto Rico and made his first appearance on record with the traditional "Cotton Mill Girls" on a Jester Records compilation. Soon he met key musical figures in his life such as John Lomax Jr., Lightnin' Hopkins, Mance Lipscomb, Jerry Jeff Walker, Gary White, Frank Davis, K.T. Oslin, and especially Townes Van Zandt. He and White, along with a recent arrival from Austin named Minor Wilson, also learned to build guitars during these years. Guy's 1966 marriage to Susan Spaw didn't last, but their son Travis Clark eventually accompanied Guy on bass when he grew up.

Guy's days in California as the 1960s gave way to the '70s were brief but highly significant. In San Francisco in 1969, Guy and Minor Wilson teamed up to build guitars and mandolins for such luminaries as Johnny Winter and the Grateful Dead's Bob Weir. That summer, Guy attended the Old Time Fiddler's Convention in Berkeley while taking LSD, an experience that led directly to the *Old No. 1* song "Nickel For The Fiddler." After a brief return to Houston, Guy returned to California in late 1970 with Susanna Talley. They rented a house just south of Los Angeles in Long Beach, where Guy got a job at a Dobro factory.

He also played occasional gigs at a handful of Southern California folk venues, including San Diego's Heritage Coffeehouse, where the doorman was a young Tom Waits. One night, Guy and Susanna were heading back to Long Beach from San Diego on Interstate 5 and Guy muttered something about hoping to get off the freeway "without getting killed or caught." He managed to write that thought on a paper sack with Susanna's eyebrow pencil, and eventually it turned into "L.A. Freeway," the best-known song on *Old No. 1*.

That song is, of course, about leaving California behind. By late 1971, Guy and Susanna were headed for Nashville, where they rode in their friend Mickey Newbury's houseboat to get married in January 1972. Publishing company Sunbury Dunbar, which was affiliated with RCA Records, had given Guy a publishing deal that helped enable the move to Music City. The first artist to cut one of Guy's songs was Harold Lee, who used "The Old Mother's Locket Trick" as the B-side of his 1972 single "Neon Lady." (Guy never released the song himself, but Waylon Jennings and Willie Nelson recorded it for their 1981 album *WWII*.)

Later that year came two more key covers of songs that would end up on *Old No. 1* when Jerry Jeff Walker recorded both "L.A. Freeway" and "That Old Time Feeling" for his self-titled album. Also released in 1972 was Townes Van Zandt's recording of "Don't Let The Sunshine Fool Ya" on *The Late Great Townes Van Zandt*. (That song initially was slated for inclusion on *Old No. 1* before some changes were made.) Early 1973 brought Guy another cut when the Everly Brothers did "A Nickel For The Fiddler" on their album *Pass the Chicken & Listen*. And later in 1973, Walker returned to Guy's songbook with "Desperados Waiting For A Train," which appeared on his landmark live album *¡Viva Terlingua!*

By the time singer Rita Coolidge (who was married to Kris Kristofferson at the time) recorded both "Desperados" and "Nickel For The Fiddler" on her 1974 album *Fall Into Spring*, followed by Johnny Cash leading off his 1975 album *Look At Them Beans* with Clark's "Texas 1947," it was clear that Guy had earned the right to put out an album of his own. The country music landscape seemed ripe for Clark's rise, as Willie Nelson and Waylon Jennings had topped the country charts with their respective 1975 albums *Red Headed Stranger* and *Dreaming My Dreams*.

Because of Guy's publishing deal with Sunbury Dunbar, parent company RCA was the natural choice to release his debut. Clark began work on *Old No. 1* — a title that Rodney Crowell says was "a play on Jack Daniel's," the Tennessee whiskey that includes the phrase "Old No. 7" on its label — in August 1974. One aborted session and several song-changes later, Clark and RCA finally got the album in stores just as Clark was turning 34 in the November 1975. Jerry Jeff Walker wrote the stream-of-consciousness liner notes that appeared on the back cover, his words wrapped around a photo of Guy and Susanna:

July 4th, 1975
To my friend while emotionally deranged

We've been down this road
Once
Or twice before
Guy Clark's first
Hmmm
I think of young ones makin' it
Too soon
While Tom Waits
Guy writes
Of old men
And old trains
And old memories
Like black & white movies
Etched
No, carved, like crow's feet
In the corners of his past
Now he'll close his eyes
And all of those faces
And places
Pass
Again
To the natural music
Of a flat-top guitar
A fiddle
A rockport jukebox
Spilling
Stories
Texas music
Good hard workin' people
Light & dark

Like the Texas skies
Always changin'
But constantly
Texas

This is not Guy's first
Nor last
Anything
He's a Sleepy-John
Who waits
Till he knows
What he knows
Then
He'll tell ya straight
Or slightly bent
If it fits
(Some things are slightly round)
(Skid ways if memory serves me)
Well,—
Anyway
this album's been a long time comin'
I, for one, have waited
Till Ol' Sleepy-John, Guy said
"All right,
Would you write my liner notes?"
And I said
(Just like I knew what we were doin')
"Sure"

May your music set you free—
Jerry Jeff Walker

CHAPTER TWO
THE SONGS

Is *Old No. 1* Guy Clark's best album? That's a subjective call, of course, but it will always hold a special place in his catalogue simply because it was his first. More significant, perhaps, is that many songs from *Old No. 1* became lifelong fixtures in his live sets. In this chapter, we'll take a closer look at each track, from the songs' origins to their prominence in Guy's repertoire and more. But first, a few thoughts from Verlon Thompson, who almost certainly has played these songs more than anyone other than Guy himself.

The two songwriters met in the mid-1980s when Thompson joined the stable of writers at CBS Songs (which had acquired Guy's original publisher, Sunbury Dunbar). "I saw him come flying into the parking lot in that old international Jeep that he used to drive; it was all rusted out," Thompson told journalist Natalie Weiner in 2024. "He had holes in his jeans, and (was) smoking a Marlboro, and had that hair blowing in the wind. He just looked like something out of a movie. I immediately made it my first priority to get to know him. It was a slow process because, honestly, I was afraid of him. He was so big and menacing-looking, you know. Even when he was smiling, his mouth turned down on both sides. It kind of looked like he was always pissed at somebody. But eventually, we heard each other playing music in the halls and in our different rooms there, and we connected."

Thompson had never heard *Old No. 1* when the two songwriters met. "I got to know Guy as a person before I really explored his music," he explains, adding that music discovery was more of a challenge in those days. "Back then you couldn't just find a YouTube or Google it or something. So it took me a while to locate a copy (of *Old No. 1*). In fact, I think I first listened to it on a reel-to-reel tape at our publishing company. I had an upstairs writing room; they would assign you a room that you could go to and work every day, and there was a reel-to-reel up there."

After he listened to *Old No. 1*, "I realized who I was dealing with," Thompson continues. "It was intimidating, actually." Soon enough, Thompson was helping Guy record his 1988 comeback album *Old Friends*. Meanwhile, as he prepared to take on the role of Clark's onstage accompanist for what turned out to be the rest of Guy's life, Thompson became fully acquainted with the material on Clark's five previous albums. Each record which followed *Old No. 1* contained a song or two that was likely to turn up in any given Guy set: "Anyhow I Love You" and the title track from 1976's *Texas Cookin'*, "Fools for Each Other" from 1978's self-titled album, "New Cut Road" and "Heartbroke" from 1981's *The South Coast Of Texas*, "The Randall Knife" from *Better Days*.

But *Old No. 1* stands out for how many of its songs became cornerstones of Guy's repertoire. "I was looking at the songs on that album, and that was our set list every night for 20 years," Thompson marvels. "We basically did almost every one of those songs. On some nights, we'd swap one out for another, because certain sets were shorter and we didn't have time for all of them. And I don't remember performing 'Nickel For The Fiddler'; maybe a couple of times. But all the other ones were requests and staples of his nightly sets." So let's go track-by-track, in sequence, for a closer look at all ten songs on *Old No. 1*.

SIDE ONE

1. "Rita Ballou" (2:49)

Tucked into the southwestern edge of the Texas Hill Country about an hour west of San Antonio, Garner State Park is a good four hours from Monahans, the West Texas town where Guy Clark was born and lived for his first dozen years. But Clark's family made summer trips there often enough that memories of dances at the park's pavilion were ingrained in his mind.

Clark biographer Tamara Saviano asked Guy about the origins of "Rita Ballou" in an April 2000 conversation at Guy's workshop that also included fellow native-Texan musician Lee Roy Parnell. "Garner State Park is right at the bottom of the Balcones Fault Line, the most beautiful part of the Hill Country I think," Parnell said. "Garner State Park is where they take a lot of the kids for church camps, all kinds of things. Spring break and summertime you go, and I'm sure a lot of first loves were there." Guy added: "I remember going there as a kid. It was a family place, a state park. They had facilities for everything. But they had this dance floor that they had dances on — very exciting. Anyway, ('Rita Ballou') was just about that scene."

There was no actual Hill Country honky-tonker named Rita Ballou, but the surname does have a connection. Martha Ballou was an English teacher at Aransas County High School, from which Guy graduated in May 1960. The previous year, he'd had a starring role in the junior class production of the play *Our Hearts Were Young and Gay*, which Ballou directed.

In 2011, Clark's close friend and collaborator Shawn Camp was paging through Guy's old notebooks of original lyrics during an interview with Saviano, and he paused to marvel at some of the words: "'How she made them trophy buckles shine, shine, shine' — that's good." He also noticed other lyrics on the page that didn't make the final cut, but nevertheless fascinated him: "'Willard's grinnin' ear to ear, and slips her a little Everclear' — man, that's beautiful stuff." (Willard, by the way, may or may not have been a real person; we could find no further interview revelations from Guy about the song's other named character.)

Guy recorded "Rita Ballou" again on his 1981 album *The South Coast Of Texas*, with Rodney Crowell producing. Vince Gill was among the musicians who appeared on that version, which ran about 20 seconds longer and featured more electric guitar and less piano. The original *Old No. 1* version was included on several RCA hits collections: 1982's *Best of Guy Clark*, 1983's *Greatest Hits* and 1997's *The Essential Guy Clark*. "Rita Ballou" fades out on *Old No. 1* but not on *The South Coast Of Texas*, reflecting Guy's increasingly discerning studio preferences. (He told producer Miles Wilkinson before they recorded *Old Friends* in 1988 that "I've got two rules: no reverb and no fades.")

2. "L.A. Freeway" (4:43)

Like many memories recalled decades later, the origin story of "L.A. Freeway" differs depending on who's telling the tale. But it all traces back to a night in Southern California in 1970 or '71. Guy recounted the story as follows in a 1996 interview with journalist Bill DeYoung:

Guy: *I was playing in a little string band, real traditional country music, not even as sophisticated as bluegrass; real old-time. We got a gig one night in San Diego in a place called Heritage Coffeehouse. Matter of fact, Tom Waits was the doorman. I had just written 'Old Time Feeling.' Anyway, we played that night and were driving back in this guy's beautiful old restored '53 Cadillac. And it's like four o'clock in the morning. We were in the back, and I just kind of dozed off and*

raised up and said, "Man, if I could just get off this L.A. freeway with-
out getting killed or caught." It just came out of my mouth. I grabbed
Susanna's eyebrow pencil and a napkin or something and wrote it
down and carried it around in my billfold until we got to Nashville."

DeYoung: *Just that line?*

Guy: *Just that line. The landlord, that was all true. Skinny Dennis*
was the bass player in the band, and I thought I'd never see him
again. He heard the song and all of a sudden I had a new best friend.
Another line in there – "Love's a gift that's truly handmade" – that
was a painting that Susanna did. It was the letters "love is a gift
that's handmade" or something like that.

DeYoung: *People who hear that song think it's from a terrible tran-*
sitional period.

Guy: *I always think of it as a transition to a better place rather than*
from a terrible place. It wasn't that bad.

Guy told some version of that story to many journalists over the
years — including Clark biographer Tamara Saviano in 2002: "It
was about four in the morning coming back from a club gig. I
was in the back of the car and I woke up to see where we were,
and I said, 'If I could just get off of this L.A. freeway without getting killed or caught." Lights are going off in my head, so I got Susanna's eyebrow pencil and a burger sack off the floor and wrote
it down and then carried it around in my wallet for a while."

Memories from his peers add some extra layers to the history. Lyle Lovett first met Guy in the mid-1980s at a restaurant in
Nashville, after Clark had heard a demo of Lovett's songs. Not
long after, Guy invited Lyle to come to his house. "He and Susanna picked me up in their Cadillac, and we drove out to their

house in Mount Juliet, the one that Townes ended up living in later," Lyle recalls. "Guy let me flip through his notebooks and I'm reading the lyrics — you know, handwritten lyrics in Guy's hand — to 'L.A. Freeway.' And I'm reading, 'If I could just get off of this Long Beach freeway without getting killed or caught.' And I said, 'So, Guy, what's up with this Long Beach?' He said, 'I lived in Long Beach at the time.' And he said, 'L.A. sang better.' And that was that."

Then there's Verlon Thompson's version, clearly based on hearing a somewhat different story directly from Guy. "When Guy and Susanna were living out there, they were actually on the freeway, and he was trying to get off," Thompson said. "He was on one of those cloverleaf kind of things, and every time he'd come to the exit, somebody would cut him off and he'd have to circle all the way around. At one point he just sort of yelled, 'You know, if I could just get off of this damn freeway without getting killed or caught.' And Susanna reaches in the back seat and grabs a burger sack and took her mascara pencil and wrote that down on the burger sack and took it home. And then it became a song. But those words were actually said on the L.A. freeway as he was trying to get off at his exit."

I tend to believe the story about returning from Heritage Coffeehouse the most, though it's entirely possible that Guy told Verlon about an incident with a cloverleaf interchange that underscored the sentiment of the chorus's key lyric. But however the inspiration struck, it was a good lesson in documenting such a moment. "If you don't write that down, you'll forget it," Guy told journalist Bob Edwards in 2010. "One of the few disciplines I employ is to really try to write stuff down. When you have that little flash, that little inspiration, if you don't write it down, you'll forget it in 30 seconds. You have to go back and try to make sense of it later, but if you don't write it down, it's gone, as far as I can tell."

A postscript: We'll look at memorable covers of *Old No. 1* songs in a later chapter, but it seems essential to mention Jerry Jeff Walker's version, as his 1972 single of "L.A. Freeway" was how many people first heard the songwriting of Guy Clark. It wasn't a chart smash — it squeaked into the *Billboard* Hot 100 at No. 98 — but it did get a good deal of airplay in several markets nationwide. As often happens with covers, slight lyric changes were made: Jerry Jeff sings "that" L.A. Freeway instead of "this"; the pink card in the third verse becomes a pink slip; and Susanna's name gets changed to a more universal "my lady." Walker also repeated the first two lines of the chorus at the end of each chorus.

One of Walker's word-changes lives on in the name of a new record label. In 2024, Guy Clark LLC, representing Guy's estate through a board of family and friends, launched Truly Handmade Records to release albums by talented singer-songwriters. On *Old No. 1*, Guy sang "Love's a gift that's surely handmade," but Jerry Jeff had sung "truly handmade" on his 1972 hit version. And then there's that now-iconic phrase in the chorus — "without getting killed or caught" — which became the title of both Tamara Saviano's 2016 biography of Clark on Texas A&M Press, and of the 2021 documentary film Saviano and Paul Whitfield made about Guy, Susanna and Townes.

3. "She Ain't Goin' Nowhere" (3:27)

In *Without Getting Killed Or Caught,* Saviano refers to this one as "Guy's favorite song he's ever written." And then she quotes his own fascinating description of the tune: "It's a three-minute song about ten seconds in a woman's life."

Steve Earle, who was 20 when he added backing vocals to *Old No. 1,* cites "She Ain't Goin' Nowhere" as his favorite song on the album. "There's something about it," he said. "And I do think that it's kind of a feminist piece, you know. None of us actually walked that as well as we talked it."

Speaking to journalist Bob Edwards in 2010, Guy said that the song "just came out almost as fast as I could write it down. Probably my favorite piece of writing because it's really succinct. There's no waste of words. There's no holes — I mean, not that there's NO holes; I like leaving holes in songs. It's like good guitar players — it's not what you play, it's the holes you leave. And the same with lyrics, I think."

Was the song written from personal experience? It's not hard to imagine the Susanna we see in the cover photo of 2012's *My Favorite Picture Of You* as having the same grit and determination of the character in "She Ain't Goin' Nowhere." Guy told journalist Brian Atkinson in 2011 that "I envisioned Susanna because she's like that. She's not scared of anything. It wasn't based on a particular incident, but just the character."

After Susanna Clark's death, while Saviano was working on the documentary film *Without Getting Killed or Caught,* Clark told Saviano he wrote the song for Susanna's sister Bunny Talley. Bunny, who was in a relationship with Guy at the time, killed herself in 1970. In one of Guy's lyric notebooks that includes "She Ain't Goin' Nowhere," Guy wrote on the same page: "Bunny Talley shot herself in the head." He told Saviano that the line "She ain't going nowhere, she's just leaving" came to him while thinking about Bunny's suicide.

4. "A Nickel for the Fiddler" (2:45)

Unlike "She Ain't Goin' Nowhere," the fourth track on side one was in fact written about a very specific event: The Old Time Fiddler's Convention at Provo Park in Berkeley, California, on June 21, 1969. An archived flyer doesn't list the performers, but the event included fiddle, banjo and band contests, with judges Jon Lundberg, Campbell Coe and John Campbell. ("Winner in each division receives a delicious homemade pie!")

Guy was living in the Bay Area that summer, making instruments with fellow Texas transplant Minor Wilson. Guy and a friend decided to check out the festival, which was broadcast live on a local FM station. "We went over there and stood around, and it was (Jefferson Airplane members) Jack Casady and Jorma (Kaukonen), and I can't remember who else was there," Guy told Tamara Saviano in May 2015. "They had this little pickup trio or (quartet) or whatever, and they were playing traditional (music). ... I just kind of enjoyed their approach to whatever they were doing. And they had this beautiful girl fiddle player — I don't know who it was, but I got a picture of her right there that somebody took. It was just charming, and I think I probably taken some acid. And I was just, 'Wow' — mesmerized. So that's what that song is about."

The acid presumably explains why the last line of the chorus follows "It's country music in the park" with "and everybody's ruined." Not "happy," or "dancing," but "ruined." And also why Guy describes the summer solstice as "a high holiday."

5. "That Old Time Feeling" (4:10)

In *Without Getting Killed or Caught*, Saviano writes that this one "was not the first song Guy ever wrote, but it is the first song he kept." In conversations Guy had with Saviano and others, he dug a little deeper in to just what that meant.

The first song he wrote, back in his 1960s Houston days, was "Step Inside My House," which remained a hidden treasure until Lyle Lovett made it the title track of his 1998 double-album focusing on material by fellow Texas singer-songwriters. "That

Old Time Feeling" dates to Guy and Susanna's Los Angeles days in 1970-71.

"I remember it was a Saturday," Guy told journalist Bill DeYoung in May 1996. "I was off work just sitting there drinking wine, and 'Old Time Feeling' just like came. I've got the original paper I wrote it on. It was like, 'All right. There's one.'" In a May 2011 interview with journalist Brian Atkinson, Guy shed a little more light on the subject, noting that he'd written about five or six songs at that point — "but 'That Old Time Feeling' is the first good song I ever wrote. ... It's still one of my favorite songs." It was one of a few songs Guy played for music publisher Sunbury Dunbar in Los Angeles in 1971, the end result of which was a publishing deal that sparked Guy and Susanna's move to Nashville. It's also worth noting that while Guy usually cited "She Ain't Goin' Nowhere" as his favorite, he gave that designation to "That Old Time Feeling" in a couple of interviews just after *Old No. 1* came out.

The best story about "That Old Time Feeling" comes from a February 2011 interview Saviano did with Guy, Shawn Camp and Steve Earle. It involves the great Tom Waits, who'd been the doorman at San Diego's Heritage Coffeehouse the night that Guy wrote the key line of "L.A. Freeway" on the drive home to Long Beach.

"I was over at Dick Feller's house one night," Guy begins. "We'd been up all night. He played me the first Tom Waits record I'd ever heard. I was just like, 'Oh man, that was so fucking...' He said, 'You want to talk to him? 'Sure.' He's like, 'He's playing tonight in Philadelphia at the Tin Angel. Let's see, what time would he get off? I know where he's staying.' He called the hotel and said, 'Is Tom Waits there?' 'No, he just walked out, but he said he'd be back in about 20 minutes.'

"So he called him back, and they talked for a while. He said, 'I want you to meet a friend of mine, Guy Clark.' I picked up the phone and said, 'Hey, man, nice to talk to you.' He goes, 'That old time feeling goes sneaking down the hall/Like an old grey cat in winter...' He recited the whole song of 'Old Time Feeling.' And that's all he said. He was the doorman at this club in San Diego when I had this string band that played there. I remember playing 'That Old Time Feeling' for the first time at that gig."

Earle then chimes in: "I heard that same story from Waits at the *Dead Man Walking* concert in 1995 or whenever it was." Camp adds: "So he remembered it?" Earle answers: "Oh, absolutely, the whole thing." Guy has the last word: "It was like, 'Wow, I have arrived.'"

SIDE TWO

6. "Texas 1947" (3:10)

Taking a close look at the rambunctious tune that kicks off the second side of *Old No. 1*, what strikes me most about "Texas 1947" — or "Texas - 1947" if you follow the exact rendering of the title as it appeared on the album jacket — is how different it is from all the other songs on the album. Indeed, it's different from most songs by anyone, in terms of the structure of the lyrics.

Guy was never really hemmed in by the verse-chorus-verse-chorus routine, as evidenced by the immediately preceding song on the album: "That Old Time Feeling" has four verses that all begin with the titular line, but no choruses. But on "Texas 1947," he really throws the rulebook out the window. Clark tends toward economy in lyrics; remember his earlier quote about leaving holes in songs. But on "Texas 1947" he comes right out of the gate with words-a-blazin'. The opening line begins just two seconds into the song, and by the 45-second mark he's given us a 118-word first verse before charging straight into another verse of 98 words. (It ain't Kendrick Lamar, but hey, for Guy, it's downright loquacious.)

Then we finally get a chorus, and an odd one it is: Three lines about the train arriving and leaving, then two more descriptive lines before repeating the first three again. And then, hanging out there all by itself after a brief instrumental interlude, the wonderful spoken line: "Lord, she never even stopped." Then one more verse — shorter this time, just 44 words — before a final chorus that repeats the three main lines until fade-out.

The song's fast pace and railroad theme (Guy learned a thing or two from "Newbury's train songs") should have made it a radio hit in a perfect world, but no songs from the album charted as singles. And yet, around the same time *Old No. 1* was arriving in record racks nationwide, so was a Johnny Cash 7-inch single of "Texas 1947," It wasn't a huge hit for Cash, but it did sneak into the *Billboard* top-40 country chart at No. 35 in January 1976.

7. "Desperados Waiting for a Train" (4:31)

If there's three or four compositions that might be considered Guy Clark's signature song, "Desperados Waiting For A Train" is inarguably one of them. (And yes, like "Texas 1947," the title was rendered slightly differently on the album jacket: "Desperados Waiting for THE train," instead of "a." Because Guy sings "a," we're going with that variation in this book.) "I knew when I finished that and played it for folks that it was something special," he told Tamara Saviano in November 2015, very near the end of his life.

"Desperados" paints a vivid picture of Jack Prigg, a family friend who became like a surrogate grandfather to Guy during his preteen years in Monahans. It's pretty much straight documentary, but with the kind of character-sketch color and poetic lyricism that mark Guy's best work. Fellow Texas songwriter

Terry Allen told me that when he first heard the song, he was impressed at how it "kind of engaged a history like that. And I think that's what really touches people about it. That's what gets me about it."

"'Desperados Waiting for a Train' was written when Guy was in his late 20s or early 30s about stuff that happened when he was eight," Steve Earle told Saviano in February 2011. "It's that kind of memory for detail and attention to detail" that sets Guy apart from most songwriters, he added. "Guy's incredibly detailed, like details within details."

As high as the song ranks in Clark's catalogue among his fans, there was one notable detractor. In her Clark biography, Saviano quotes Susanna Clark recalling that "when Guy sang 'Desperados Waiting for a Train" for Townes, [Townes] said, 'Gone commercial, huh?' I remember that because Guy repeated a chorus and Townes was like, 'For God's sake, you don't repeat a chorus over and over again.'"

Repeating choruses in a song is not all that unusual, of course — essentially, that's what a chorus is — but "Desperados" stands out because the chorus consists only of the song's title line. Guy sings the line twice in the first four choruses, and four times at the end. I'll cut Townes a little slack here and say that the repetition never quite sat well with me, either. But I've certainly never interpreted it as a sign of Guy being motivated by commercial concerns. Rather, that one line is like a mantra, almost a spiritual chant at the core of the song.

8. "Like a Coat From the Cold" (3:18)

By Guy's standards, "Like A Coat From the Cold" is a fairly straightforward love ballad, with two autobiographical verses about Guy's wild streak balanced against a chorus that reveals his love for Susanna with the title metaphor. It's arguably the most middle-of-the-road musical arrangement as well, with tasteful piano runs that set the tone atop gentle acoustic guitar picking.

Speaking with Saviano in June 2015, Texas songwriter Ray Wylie Hubbard remembers it as being the first Guy Clark song he ever heard, using the words "envy" and "jealousy" to describe his reaction. "I think it was down here in Austin," he continued. "We were at some party ... I think Jerry Jeff was there. It was just one of those passing-the-guitar-around (parties), and I think Guy sang 'Coat From the Cold.' Everybody picked up their jaws off the floor. Nobody wanted to follow."

The only prominent artist who's covered it on an album is Jerry Jeff Walker, who included it on his 1975 album *Ridin' High*, released a few weeks before *Old No. 1*. The most interesting part about that story is where Walker learned the song: in Barbados, while on his honeymoon with Susan Walker in 1974. Halfway through the honeymoon, Guy and Susanna flew down to join the festivities, at Jerry Jeff's invitation. Given that Townes Van Zandt lived for months with newlyweds Guy and Susanna in 1972, it seems fair enough for Guy and Susanna to crash Jerry Jeff and Susan Walker's honeymoon.

"I picked them up in the car and we went over and stayed in the house," Walker recalled in a June 2013 interview with Saviano. "We had a pretty good time. In fact, while we were there, I learned "Coat From the Cold." Guy had just written it." Fittingly, Walker adds, the song has "kind of become more peoples' honeymoon song or wedding song than any other one."

9. "Instant Coffee Blues" (3:15)

When asked about "Instant Coffee Blues," several of Guy's peers made a similar observation — that the song plays out like a short film. It recounts a one-night stand and the morning after, a situation plenty of listeners could identify with.

"I've always thought that was one of the best songs that I wrote," Guy told Saviano in December 2010. "For years and years, that was the only song people consistently requested. No matter where you go, somebody's gonna ask from the audience, 'Instant Coffee Blues.' For a long time, I knew it cold and would play it anytime anyone would ask for it. That was kind of a breakthrough in writing."

Nashville singer-songwriter Brennen Leigh, who got to know Clark in his later years, cites "Instant Coffee Blues" as a song that taught her some lessons about writing. "He was able to make a mundane human interaction magical," Leigh told journalist Natalie Weiner in 2024. "I'm going to use 'Instant Coffee Blues' as an example. This girl picks up this guy at a bar, and then he goes home in the morning. And the whole interaction is just beautiful, from start to finish, every little nuance. He made the mundane, or what appeared to be mundane, not mundane. He made it poetry."

We'll give the last word on this one to Verlon Thompson. "The one (from *Old No. 1*) that stood out to me, and still does to this day, is 'Instant Coffee Blues.' It's a Hollywood movie in three minutes," he told Weiner in 2024. "You don't know the characters' names or anything, and you don't really know what happened before or after. But you're drawn into that moment they come together, and then the moment they part. 'She just had to go to work, and he just had to go.' And 'he knew how to blow it off.' And she's sitting at the stoplight, touching up her face, and he's got his memories in his guitar case. Those images really stuck with me. To this day, I still don't think anyone's handled that moment in a relationship — or not a relationship, whatever it was — nobody's handled it quite that way. It's still dignified, in a way. Nobody's right or wrong. It doesn't seem like anything wrong has happened. It's just this meeting. And then there's the reality of it, you know. That's a tough subject to handle in a song and make it entertaining and enjoyable. "

10. "Let Him Roll" (4:05)

If it's not quite as prominent as "Desperados Waiting For A Train" and "L.A. Freeway" in the Guy Clark songbook, "Let Him Roll" is pretty close. It's also hugely important simply because it provided the fingerpicking musical structure that Guy basically duplicated a few years later for "The Randall Knife," arguably his finest lyrical composition. ("I try not to do 'The Randall Knife' and 'Let Him Roll' in the same set because the music is just identical," Clark told Tamara Saviano in December 2010.)

"Let Him Roll" might be Guy's finest hour as a fictional storyteller. Unlike highwater marks such as "Desperados" or "The Randall Knife" or "My Favorite Picture Of You," all drawn directly from Guy's own experiences, this one "wasn't literally about any one character," he told Saviano in July 2014. "It was a conglomeration."

That said, during a previous interview with Saviano in December 2010, he got a little more specific. "There was this old wino who hung out at a place called the Old Quarter in Houston where Townes and I and a bunch of people played. It was loosely built around him," Guy said. "He was the elevator man at the hotel down the street. I allowed myself artistic or theatrical license, I guess, to write this story around it, using him as the character in my head."

One of the most colorful details in Saviano's book *Without Getting Killed Or Caught* is the revelation that Guy wrote it one day in 1972 after nailing himself in the bedroom of the house he shared with his wife Susanna and, for the first year of their marriage, Townes Van Zandt. "It all involved alcohol, I'm sure," Guy told Saviano in an interview for the book. "Something pissed me off about the way Townes and Susanna were denigrating my intelligence, and I was offended."

Musically, Guy's guide for the spoken-word-over-finger-picking construction was Ramblin' Jack Elliott, and specifically Jack's song "912 Greens," an account of a 1953 visit to New Orleans with two friends (one of whom, ironically, was named Guy). "He got that (guitar part) from trying to learn '912 Greens' from Jack Elliott," longtime accompanist Verlon Thompson told journalist Natalie Weiner in 2024. "It morphed a little bit, but that pattern was what 'Let Him Roll' is based on. Guy was really influenced by, as he used to say, the folk scare of the '60s."

The song has no chorus and eleven (!) verses — or ten, if you count the final verse as the chorus, as that's where he finally goes from speaking to singing and cites the song's title line. Spoiler alert: The main character dies about two-thirds of the way through, but what happens at his funeral is really the crux of the song. Lyle Lovett, speaking in July 2025, summed up the song's value succinctly: "'Let Him Roll' is life and death and everything in between, and everything you need. There's only one song in the whole world that could be that one."

CHAPTER THREE
OLD NO. 1, TAKE ONE

One of the most intriguing and consequential details about the making of *Old No. 1* is that the album everyone heard when it was released in November 1975 was quite different than the album Guy Clark initially recorded more than a year earlier. The sessions for that version were done at Nashville's storied RCA Studio A in August 1974.

Guy's record deal with RCA Records came together largely because he had been a staff writer for several years at Sunbury Dunbar, a publishing company that RCA owned at the time. In the fall of 1971, Guy played four songs for Gerry Teifer, who headed Sunbury Dunbar's Los Angeles office, and Teifer was impressed enough to offer Clark a deal on the spot. A $500 advance helped Guy and Susanna move from Long Beach to Nashville.

As other artists began cutting Guy's songs — Jerry Jeff Walker, Rita Coolidge, the Everly Brothers and Johnny Cash among them — it became increasingly obvious that a Guy Clark album should happen. His deal with Sunbury Dunbar gave RCA the inside track. Mike Lipskin, an RCA staff producer based in New York, liked what he heard of Guy's songs and offered him a record deal.

Guy traveled to New York, had dinner with Lipskin and discussed the deal in Lipskin's office. "And I said, before I sign you, this is a very important point to me: You have to agree to use the Memphis sound and the people that had been part of Chips Moman's rhythm section," Lipskin told me in August 2025. "And he said, 'That's fine.'"

On the surface, this seemed like a good plan. Clark and Moman were friends; in fact, in August 1973 Guy and Susanna had been at a party at Moman's studio on Music Row the night before they headed to the tiny Texas town of Luckenbach. At the party, Guy explained the lure of the hill country hamlet to Moman, and the next day Moman co-wrote "Luckenbach, Texas (Back to the Basics of Love)" with musician Bobby Emmons. Four years later, Waylon Jennings' recording of the song (with Willie Nelson guesting) spent a month atop the *Billboard* country charts.

Emmons, in fact, was one of Moman's legendary backing crew at American Sound Studios, collectively known as the Memphis Boys. "Mike Leech was the one who pulled together all the musicians," Lipskin said of the bassist who'd played on late-1960s Memphis classics by Elvis Presley and Dusty Springfield, among countless others. From the Memphis Boys crew, Leech brought along organist Emmons, guitarist Reggie Young and pianist Bobby Wood. Other aces came from Muscle Shoals, including drummer Jerry Carrigan and horn players Harrison Calloway, Harvey Lee Thompson and Charles Rose.

Lipskin says the recording process took about a week, but that problems developed because Guy "had a time problem, one of the worst time problems I've ever encountered. His guitar wouldn't keep with his voice when he was with the rock-steady rhythm section. So I had to hire another guitar player to play his parts. And he was very, very upset. He said, what will my fans think? I said, 'Unfortunately, that's the way it has to be,' because it would be an absolute mess if he had played rhythm guitar."

Guy's take on the problems with the session was, not surprisingly, rather different. "The producer pissed me off," Guy told Tamara Saviano in an interview for *Without Getting Killed or Caught*. "I walked into the studio one day and found he'd flown in an entire horn section to play on my record. The charts had been written and the session planned out without asking me anything. It would have been an absolute disaster had I put that record out."

Guy's comments were somewhat more diplomatic in a 1976 interview with journalist Pete Oppel for *The Dallas Morning News.* "I recorded it once and then scratched it," he said of *Old No. 1.* "It just wasn't right. That first effort was a learning process and after listening to it I just realized the record had to be done over. It was my decision and I told my manager and he told the record company. It was a very obvious thing that the album wasn't right. I just communicated the songs the wrong way. I changed my entire attitude. I was more relaxed the second time."

The bottom line may have been as simple as this: Just because the band Lipskin assembled was first-rate didn't mean it was the right fit for Clark's artistic vision. A prevailing thread throughout much of Saviano's biography is that Guy spent the first decade of his recording career mostly not liking the records he made — even one produced by Rodney Crowell, one of Guy's closest friends and colleagues. Guy generally didn't care for drums on his records, probably because he considered himself first and foremost a folkie. "Guy had been writing and playing for a decade," Saviano writes in chapter seven of *Without Getting Killed or Caught.* "He knew who he was as an artist. Guy was a folksinger. He favored stripped-down, acoustic instrumentation with the vocals up front and lyrics playing a starring role on the recordings."

The problem was that Guy had agreed up-front to Lipskin's terms of aiming for the "Memphis sound" on the album. "It only happened after we heard the finished product that he and his wife didn't like it," Lipskin says. Two observations about this: First, because Guy had never recorded an album before, it's understandable that he might not have fully grasped how different Lipskin's approach would be from how Guy envisioned his songs would sound. Second, and perhaps more important: This was Guy's first chance at getting a record of his own out into the world. To have pre-emptively declined Lipskin's offer because he was concerned about the recording details would have been a major sacrifice on Guy's part. Who knows how much longer it might have taken him to get a record deal?

Michael Brovsky, whose Free Flow Productions company managed Guy from the mid-'70s to the early '80s, dealt with RCA brass over how to proceed. "At the end of the day, what he (Lipskin) was coming up with just wasn't right," Brovsky told Saviano in April 2015. "There was a substantial amount of money spent on that first version. And it was my job to go and say, 'Listen, we're not happy with this.' I had the power to do that because of the production company, so I said, 'We're going to start all over, different studio, different everything.'"

The restart was actually documented in the press as it was happening. A publication called *The Southern Voice* featured an October 1974 column by Nashville writer and historian John Lomax that began as follows: "Dash it all, you have to wait a little bit longer to hear Guy Clark's debut album. RCA has signed him, an album was recorded, the artwork was completed, but mixing problems developed. A new producer is being engaged to salvage the tapes. This will probably mean recutting some new songs. The record was scheduled for November (1974) issue, my guess is that it will now emerge to brighten the new year. At this point it looks as if Neil Wilburn will take over. He's an excellent engineer and producer who has worked well with Guy in the past and is very familiar with his music."

Another factor in the big picture of Guy's RCA deal was that Mike Berniker, the company's recently-installed A&R chief, was not a fan. Berniker made his name producing early Barbra Streisand records and wasn't particularly well-versed in folk troubadours. "I had signed Guy Clark before he became head of

A&R," Lipskin says, "and he didn't think Guy Clark could sing, because he had no feeling or understanding for Guy Clark's brilliance as a composer. I really think that Guy Clark just had stupendous lyrics and phrasing, and his whole thing is just beautiful."

I asked Lipskin if, in retrospect, he wished he had not made the signing contingent upon the "Memphis sound" approach. What if Guy had said that he wanted the record deal but not Lipskin's studio plan? "I first would have said, 'Well, let's do half the songs the way you want in the in the older country style, and then do at least five of them the way I want to do them," he replied. "And if he said no, I would have said, 'Well, I don't think you're going to sell many records. I'll be glad to produce it and you do the choosing of it, but I really don't think it's going to be that commercial."

Perhaps it was as predictable as that: The record label prioritized commercial concerns, while Guy prioritized his art above all else. As he told Saviano in *Without Getting Killed or Caught*: "I never did write songs for country radio. I wasn't a country singer and am still not a country singer. I just write songs and play them. I'm Guy Clark. My songs are not really geared to sell a lot of records and have hits. I just do what I do."

This certainly wasn't the first time that a musician felt the results in the studio did not reflect his own artistic identity. But an intriguing parallel could be drawn between *Old No. 1* and the self-titled Atlantic Records debut of *John Prine*, released four years earlier. Although Prine recorded in Memphis at Chips Moman's American Sound Studios rather than in Nashville, he and Clark were in surprisingly similar situations with their respective debuts. Both wanted to put their best foot forward on their first album, and both were fundamentally folk singer-songwriters without much experience playing with bands behind them.

And, as it happens, they recorded largely with the same band. Author Erin Osmon, writing about Prine's now-classic

1971 debut album for Bloomsbury Academic Publishing's 33-1/3 book series, details how Jerry Wexler signed Prine to Atlantic Records with a plan for him to work in Memphis with accomplished producer Arif Mardin. The musicians included bassist Mike Leech, lead guitarist Reggie Young, organist Bobby Emmons, and pianist Bobby Wood — all of whom joined Clark for Lipskin's *Old No. 1* sessions three years later.

"If it seems like The Memphis Boys and the Memphis sound didn't have much in common with the spare, pensive story-songs of John Prine, it's because they didn't," Osmon writes in chapter ten. "With Prine, there was nary a groove to be found. And when he stepped into the studio in July of 1971 the contrast was quickly apparent. 'We would cut blues, heavy R&B, pop, rock and roll, and our version of country,' said Bobby Wood, who played piano on *John Prine*. 'Folk music is really light, not heavy. We weren't good at light. ... We were on totally unfamiliar ground.'"

Their experience with Prine, and other songwriters they backed in the ensuing couple of years, likely made them far better at working with folk songwriters by the time they joined Clark and Lipskin in the studio. But if the Memphis Boys were still finding their way with country-folk troubadours in 1971, Prine decided he could abide by the results. "Wood remembered Prine as quiet and respectful," Osmon noted in her book. "There was no feeling of tension despite the oil-and-water quality of the songs and the session players. 'We just went to work doing what we always do, trying to find some kind of identity,' he said. ... Prine later revealed his mindset. 'Scared of the studio,' he said. 'Scared of the musicians. You can't tell guys that play 200 times better than yourself they're doing something wrong.'"

And, much like *Old No. 1*, Prine's debut moved slowly at first — it peaked at No. 154 on the *Billboard* pop albums chart in 1972 — but eventually became regarded as an American classic. Amazingly, after Prine's death in 2020, his debut album re-entered the

Billboard 200 at No. 55 — its highest chart position coming nearly five decades after it was released. *Old No. 1* didn't make the *Billboard* pop chart; it reached No. 41 on the country chart, and then its reputation gradually grew as Guy continued to build his career.

But the difference in the arrangements is only one aspect of how the released album changed from what Lipskin had recorded. When Guy reconvened with Neil Wilburn, who'd engineered his demos, to remake the album, he also swapped out half of the songs. This clearly had nothing to do with Lipskin and Clark's different visions; Guy had signed off on all ten songs recorded for the Lipskin version. So why the changes in material?

Saviano speculates, based on conversations with Guy, that because the redone version relied heavily on demos Guy had done with Wilburn, he maybe "didn't have quality enough demos of the other songs to put on *Old No. 1*," she notes. It's also possible, as Lipskin guesses, that the initial sessions might have changed Guy's mind about which songs were best for his debut album. "When you mix down and add different parts to any recording, it's going to change your opinion over a certain period of time," Lipskin said.

Whatever the reasons, I'd contend that the final version of *Old No. 1* raised the bar in terms of Guy's songwriting. Here's how it breaks down:

— Songs on both versions: "L.A. Freeway," "That Old Time Feeling," "Desperados Waiting for a Train," "Like a Coat From the Cold," "Let Him Roll."
— Songs on Lipskin's version, but not on the final album: "Don't Let The Sunshine Fool You," "Virginia's Real," "The Ballad Of Laverne and Captain Flint," "Anyhow I Love You," "It's About Time."
— Songs on the final album, but not on Lipskin's version: "Rita Ballou," "She Ain't Goin' Nowhere," "Texas 1947," "A Nickel for the Fiddler," "Instant Coffee Blues."

In retrospect, it's hard to fathom that Guy would not have put "She Ain't Goin' Nowhere," which he considered the best song he ever wrote, on his debut. It's also difficult to imagine side two of *Old No. 1* not kicking off with the live-wire excitement of "Texas 1947." Furthermore, as both Guy and Verlon Thompson have noted, "Instant Coffee Blues" became the one song they could always count on receiving an audience request at their shows, decades into the future. And "Rita Ballou" struck just the right tone as the album opener. Only "A Nickel for the Fiddler" seems a slight surprise among the additions; sticking with "Anyhow I Love You" might have been more apropos.

But it wasn't like Guy had soured on the five songs he discarded from the Lipskin sessions. Four of them ended up being re-recorded for Guy's second album, 1976's *Texas Cookin'* — so it clearly wasn't a case of Guy just deciding he didn't like those tunes. (The other song, "Don't Let The Sunshine Fool Ya," was also redone for *Texas Cookin'* but didn't make it onto the album; it finally surfaced in 1997 as part of an RCA compilation called *The Essential Guy Clark*.)

For all the drama surrounding the way the two versions of the album differed in sound, it's ultimately the material that makes or breaks a record. Much as *John Prine* succeeded first and foremost because it included a handful of songs that became standards — "Angel From Montgomery," "Hello in There," "Sam Stone," "Paradise," "Illegal Smile" — so did *Old No. 1* rest its laurels on a similarly impressive track list of undeniably great songs: "L.A. Freeway," "Desperados Waiting for a Train," "Texas 1947," "She Ain't Goin' Nowhere," "Let Him Roll."

"I've been a producer, and it really is about songs," Steve Earle told journalist Natalie Weiner in 2024. "How are you going to fuck that up? They could have put out the first one (Lipskin's version), and it would have been fine, you know? But the point is, if he was going to make a record with horns and stuff, he could have stayed in L.A. and done that. Guy's reasoning for being moved to Nashville when he signed his deal was to get around players like that."

If Guy held any grudges about the aborted initial session, he didn't stress it when the two musicians encountered each other in San Francisco years later, Lipskin says. After he left his job with RCA, Lipskin returned to his love of playing stride jazz piano; he still appears semi-regularly in the Bay Area. He had begun a long-running residency at a San Francisco venue when, sometime in the 1980s, Clark was playing in town (probably at Great American Music Hall) and stopped by Lipskin's gig.

"I think we had a drink," Lipskin recalls. "And I said, you know, I'm very sorry the way our situation turned out with that record, because I still think you're extremely brilliant as a composer. And he said, 'Aw, don't worry about it.'"

Whatever Guy's experience with Lipskin may have been in the studio, one thing is indisputable: The simple fact that Lipskin signed Clark to his first record deal makes him an important figure in Guy's career. Though it took time for *Old No. 1* to evolve into what it finally became, the bottom line is that RCA ultimately introduced Guy Clark to the world.

CHAPTER FOUR
OLD NO. 1, TAKE TWO

After Guy Clark rejected the results of producer Mike Lipkin's August 1974 sessions at RCA Studio A, he turned to Plan B — which, fittingly, was in part to use RCA Studio B, a smaller Nashville studio owned by the label. That's where Guy went in early 1975 to remake *Old No. 1* with Neil Wilburn, who had engineered publishing demos Guy made before the Lipskin sessions. The idea was to use those demos as the foundation for the album, with overdubs added to flesh out the arrangements. They also worked at a new Nashville location of Chips Moman's American Sound Studios, as Moman had recently relocated from Memphis to Nashville. (The Nashville location was renamed American Studios.)

Wilburn was ultimately a better fit for Clark's music. He hadn't yet done much producing — in 1970, he and Charlie Daniels teamed up to co-produce albums for Ramblin' Jack Elliott and Gary & Randy Scruggs — but his credits as an engineer were impressive. They included Bob Dylan's *Nashville Skyline*, Leonard Cohen's *Songs From a Room*, Michael Murphey's *Geronimo's Cadillac* and the Byrds' *Dr. Byrds & Mr. Hyde*.

Maybe most important, he and Guy had become comfortable with each other. "Neil had been engineering demos I had done for the publishing company, and I just liked what he was doing," Guy told Tamara Saviano in chapter seven of *Without Getting Killed or Caught*. "He knew how to get the right sound, and he liked my songs, which is a pretty good start for a working relationship."

Any chance to interview Wilburn about the sessions ended in 1990, when he died of a heart attack at age 56. But another key player at the sessions was Pat Carter, the head of Sunbury Dunbar publishing and a musician himself. Carter is listed as a guitarist and harmony vocalist on the record, but more intriguing is this additional credit: "Texas 1947, She Ain't Goin' Nowhere, Instant Coffee Blues and Rita Ballou were produced in association with Pat Carter & Sunbar Productions." In a 2024 interview, journalist Natalie Weiner spoke with Carter, who now lives in Santa Fe, about his role in making *Old No. 1*.

"I had hired Neil to engineer all of our demos for the publishing company, and all of these songs that were on the *Old No. 1* album I had already done demos on," Carter said. Those demos included contributions from some of the same players who took part in the Lipskin sessions, including guitarist Reggie Young, bassist Mike Leech and drummer Jerry Carrigan. "There were some great musicians on there," he continued. "Of course Johnny Gimble was one of the great fiddle players in the world; he's gone now. Almost all these guys are gone ... but we had some great musicians. David Briggs, who was Elvis's piano player, did most of the piano work on it." Briggs died of cancer in April 2025.

"Because I'd used all these great musicians, they were great demos," Carter said. "They sounded like masters. But Neil wanted to redo all of them, which was fine. We went in and recut all of them. We did almost all of them at American (Sound) Studios, which was down 16th Street. We tried to do some overdubs in RCA (Studio) B, but not much of it worked. ... There were several of them that we just couldn't get the feel that we had on the demos. So they took our tracks that we had done as demos, and just remixed them and added a few things and used those on the album." (Those are the four songs for which Carter received "produced in association with" credit.)

"We used a lot of different musicians on the demos," Carter added. "There's so many sessions (in Nashville) that you can't always get the same people, so you had to do what you could. There's a guy Dick Feller, who was a buddy of Guy's, and he was a good acoustic player. He came in and did one little solo thing on 'Rita Ballou,' but that's all he played on. I mean, he wasn't in the studio 15 minutes. Guy was buddies of all these guys, like Mickey Raphael, who's Willie Nelson's harmonica player. He had him come in and just do a few licks. So it's not like they were there for a whole three-hour session or something."

The credits on the back cover of *Old No. 1* identify 25 total participants. But unlike Guy's next album, 1976's *Texas Cookin'*, which detailed the credits for each song, it's a guessing-game as to exactly how much each musician contributed to *Old No. 1*. More than half of those who played on the album are no longer living, and several who are still around couldn't remember exactly which tracks they played on. In addition to the musicians already noted above, the contributors included drummers Larrie Londin and Jerry Kroon; guitarists Steve Gibson, Jim Colvard and Chip Young (as well as Guy himself); keyboardists Lea Jane Berinati, Shane Keister and Chuck Cochran; Jack Hicks on dobro; and Hal Rugg on dobro and pedal steel. Harmony vocalists included Rodney Crowell, Emmylou Harris, Steve Earle, Gary B. White, Florence Warner and Sammi Smith. Berinati and Carter also added harmony vocals in addition to their instrumental contributions.

"The vibes at the sessions were wonderful," Carter continued. "Neil Wilburn was a wonderful engineer. He had a lot of good ideas that sparked good feelings on the sessions, and got some different kind of feels on stuff. It was a wonderful experience. ... Guy would bring in all of his buddies, like (Texas fiddle legend) Johnny Gimble. And, of course, luckily, Emmylou (Harris) was on there, Rodney (Crowell), people who were just buddies of his, and Steve Earle. And so the mix between the professional session musicians and the artists Guy knew was a really good blend. We all had a good time. I can't remember one cross word or anything going on that messed any of those sessions up. That *Old No. 1* album was a great experience."

In addition to her conversation with Carter, journalist Natalie Weiner spoke with eight others who played on the sessions. What follows are excerpts from those interviews, which were done for the specific purpose of this book.

RODNEY CROWELL (backing vocals)

Natalie: ***How did you first get to know Guy?***

I first got to know Guy when I had a house on Acklen Avenue in Hillsboro Village in Nashville where I was roommates with Skinny Dennis Sanchez and Richard Dobson. I had a job washing dishes, and that's how I merited a bed. I think I paid the rent all the time we were there. Those guys didn't work. Day and night, that house was always full of songwriters and what have you. (One night) I came in and I met Susanna, and we hit it off right away. But I kind of went around the corner, looked into my room there, and Guy was passed out face down in the bed with a pair of boots hanging off the end. Susanna came around the corner said, 'Yeah, that's Guy. You'll get to know him.' That was the first time. It was love at first sight.

Around what year was this?

It was '72. Fall of '72 going into '73. A lot of the songs that became *Old No. 1* were songs that I first heard either on Acklen Avenue or out at the lake. Guy and Susanna had a house on the lake next door to Mickey Newbury's houseboat. So that was a destination on Old Hickory Lake.

What was your initial impression of those songs?

As they say in the British Isles, gobsmacked. I was 22 years old, and I didn't know I was going to be a songwriter. I just thought I was a guy who'd do a lot of cover songs. ... But when you hear 'L.A. Freeway' and 'Old Time Feeling' and (Townes Van Zandt's) "Pancho & Lefty" and "No Place to Fall" and songs like that, and you're two feet from them — that changed my life forever. Because until then, I had this glib notion about playing guitars and singing. Mainly, I just did it so I could find a girlfriend. But when I heard what those guys were doing, it got my attention. That was the beginning of my becoming a songwriter. And I took it to heart. I mean, we were drinking and smoking a lot of dope, but I sobered up in a hurry when I heard those songs.

Do you recall any details of the session, or just the ambience?

I just remember it was the first record I ever sang on. I remember clearly hearing the songs for the first time more than I do the actual recording. The vibe was, "Hey Guy's recording in the studio, let's go! A bunch of hangers-on are going to come and make noise and carouse." Other artists would close sessions, but Guy welcomed it. So yeah, we would go in there and bug the producer. He didn't want to throw Guy's friends out, but he should have.

Do you have a favorite song from the album?

"Old Time Feeling" is a particularly memorable song. I remember right where I was sitting when I heard it, around the first time I first heard "Pancho & Lefty." I was stunned by the beauty and the elegance. Guy was a very elegant artist. He's a rounder and a carouser and a handful at times, but his artistic sensibilities were very elegant. I think it's one of the things that I admired the most, and tried to emulate.

And he was a great song actor. The way he would write, and the way he would emphasize what he was saying, was something I was so, so drawn to, and tried to learn by osmosis. But all of that was close to the street. The beauty of Guy Clark, and that particular time when there were so many people coming through, was that a pretty high level of art was available. You could experience it one-on-one. That's one of the beautiful things that, certainly in my formative years, Guy was particularly good at — creating a very artistic environment that was accessible if you only had two dollars in your pocket.

I consider myself lucky that I stumbled in, as an innocent child practically, into this culture. The living conditions were not refined, but the artistic intentions were. And I think that was a lovely thing to experience. I haven't listened to *Old No. 1* in a long time... but it's a testament, that record. It pointed to possibilities. Townes had (a few) records out at the time, and John Prine was already vaunted, with Kris Kristofferson on that level. But what later became Americana — I haven't really thought this through, but it just seems like the first seeds of Americana were kind of happening around '72 and '73 in Nashville, at Bishop's Pub, where high-minded songwriting was a dream that was slowly coming true.

It should be said that Guy's audience of one was Susanna. And I also learned that from Guy too. It's like early on in my songwriting, my goal, more than getting Guy's approval, was to get Susanna's approval, because if she thought your song was worthwhile, you were on your way somewhere. She was very much a part of that record.

Did you have a sense of how long the album's impact would last?

When you're working on something and you're in the middle of it, as it's happening, nothing else exists. And then once a piece of art is made and it's out — you know, I probably dined out on my name being on the on the back of a record for the first time. But we were all really busy and writing songs and going on to the next thing. So it wasn't like, hey, how many records did you sell this week on it? And that kind of thing. That never even came up. Guy was already on to the next thing he was doing, and I'd gone to California and was touring around with Emmy. This art that we make, this music stuff, it's day to day. It really is day to day. And I think for me, if it becomes anything else, the cart's either ahead of the horse or beside the horse, or something. The carrot needs to stay out in front of the horse, is what it is. And in the Guy Clark school of songwriting, the carrot was always out in front.

LEA JANE BERINATI (backing vocals, electric piano)

How did you get involved in the Old No. 1 sessions?

I was a secretary at Columbia Records, and Neil Wilburn was an engineer there. He knew I wanted to be a background singer, and he was training me with that. I'd wanted to do that since I was 11. So I really was blessed to be able to work with Guy, and his music turned out to be my favorite of 45 years singing in Nashville.

He's not country. He wasn't country. And although he was sort of thrown into the outlaw group, he really wasn't part of the outlaw group, either. But he was good friends with all of them. … There was so much talent coming out of Texas in that field, but there was something different about Guy's writing that set him apart, even from all of those. He had been compared briefly with Kristofferson, and they might be similar in some ways, but not all of them.

Guy's music was so intricate, it was almost like poetry. Down to earth, at the same time thoughtful, authentic, and he told real life stories in a way that I've never heard them done. And I can remember them years later. When we were playing this album a couple of weeks ago, I could remember every single background part that I did. I sang along with it. I even did the little licks that I had done, trying to be a little unique. And I have notes. I went back and found my booking book from 1975.

What dates were you in the studio?

May 1, 1975, we did "L.A. Freeway." At that point, Susanna told me it was a true story about them leaving L.A., and that was a charmed story. She told me about how much they didn't care for their landlord. But we also did "Old Time Feeling" on that date, and that was at RCA Studio B. Then, let's see, we also did "Desperados Waiting for a Train." And that's when Guy told me, like he did the writer of that book *Without Getting Killed or Caught,* he said, "That was actually my grandmother's boyfriend I wrote that about."

The sessions were memorable, and I'll tell you too that I am probably known for being a perfectionist twit, when it comes to chords and chord changes and harmony parts, because I do hear the notes in the chord. They call it perfect pitch; it means that if you play a piano note, I can tell you what it is without looking at the piano. Which is a great advantage if you want to know what key your refrigerator's in, but nobody really cares about that. It did help me, though, in doing arrangements. I always wrote out core charts for those sessions that I did.

I sang these sessions a lot of times with Emmylou Harris and Rodney Crowell and me doing backup. I remember that we sat at separate microphones and sang whenever we felt like it. We did not rehearse, ever, the parts, that I can recall; somehow, from the heart, they just came. I probably did some overdubbing on *Old No. 1*, but I didn't write it out. And that's a miracle for me, because if I do 'You Are My Sunshine,' I'm going to write out the notes, and all the harmony parts. No — Guy's music just calls people to the front line, and you just do it. You do it from your heart, probably because HE did."

I know I played electric piano. Whenever you hear an electric (piano), that would be something I did. That's the only instrument I played, and then I sang. But when my husband Dale and I listened to this album recently and we hit "Desperados Waiting for a Train," I looked over at Dale, and he actually had tears rolling down his face. And I said, "What touched you so much about that song?" He said, "The guy is dying." And I said, "Yeah, I know he's dying. But they were in the kitchen dreaming up their old memories of how he used to wait for the train and all that, and like they were cowboys." He said, "No, the train is death, and it's coming to get him." And I said, "Oh, I didn't realize that until now." And then I had tears. So Guy's song took on a depth that I hadn't even known about.

Every line did dream up a picture of some sort, and there were no trite words. When I heard his songs for the first time, I do remember this: Every word meant something. And it was not the ordinary way you would say it. Yet he was talking about an ordinary situation, but he described it poetically to the point that it wasn't beyond your understanding, but it was different from a lot of the country stuff that was on the radio. ... I worked with Elvis, but I have never loved music like this. I've remembered it 50 years.

EMMYLOU HARRIS (backing vocals)

Do you remember the vibe of the Old No. 1 sessions?

Oh, it was just so much fun. I mean, there's nothing better than, you know what Willie Nelson says, the life I love is making music with my friends. And that can be on the road, but it can also be in the studio. And I think that (session) could be the poster child for making music with my friends in the studio for me. "Old Time Feeling" was one of those songs that just captured something so special. We weren't really old friends at that point. We became old friends over the years. We were still pretty young, but that feeling of friendship that gives you so much in your life, Guy really captured it.

"Texas Cookin'" was on the next album, right? They sort of blend together because it was the same kind of joyous feeling of making music and all those great songs. And Rodney and Guy and Susanna and all the people around them. There was a lot of humor, you know? It just was a really enjoyable experience.

What, for you, is the impact of Old No. 1 on music in general?

I think that really Guy and Townes, Rodney, Susanna — they kind of set a standard for a new kind of song. It was sort of country, it was sort of folk, but it was new. They were not exactly inventing a new kind of music, but they were bringing things into the songs and the music of that time, from their own sense of poetry. And I think it ended up inspiring a lot of artists who came after them. I guess you could say it was the beginning of what ended up being called Americana. But really, we were all out there, sort of playing left field. We had a small audience, but an audience that would stay with us all the way.

When it was released, it's not like it was an instant number one or anything like that.

No it wasn't. But it started something. It was a seed for something that grew pretty mighty. ... Guy was incredibly important to me as an inspiration and as a person. It's hard for me to imagine my life in general, or my life as an artist without Guy.

JERRY KROON (drums)

How did you get involved in the Old No. 1 sessions?

Neil Wilburn kind of started my career in Nashville recording, and he wanted to use me. Of course, there were other drummers (on the album). There was Larrie Londin, who was a great friend of mine, and Jerry Carrigan. I was just starting to do publishing demos. And then I started doing a few more custom sessions. So I'd say Neil Wilburn was the main reason I got on that project. I didn't know much about Guy. I don't think we really knew what to expect when we got there. It was pretty exciting, but I don't think anybody expected it to have the impact that it did.

The whole thing was that it was always about the artist. But in this particular case, you're (working with) somebody who really doesn't need a band to make the song happen. I mean, Guy by himself, he's an excellent musician, in the voice inflections and the way he presents his material. So I think the main thing, as a percussionist or a drummer on this session, was how to stay out of the way of his lyric and what he's trying to say, but still provide the company that's needed for that song.

There were still a lot of times (when I was) like, oh my God, what am I doing here? What am I going to do? I want to be very respectful, because Guy is a prolific writer, and obviously peo-ple have loved him for a long time, and he's had a lot of covers of his songs. But it was such a different kind of thing than doing your standard country stuff. It wasn't straight ahead. You had to really be careful not to play something that didn't fit, and at the same time, you just really had to pay a lot of attention. But it was very chaotic at times, because there were a lot of people hanging around. It's like it was an organized party.

I don't remember how many sessions I did, but I was on a lot of the album. It was nerve wracking for me, because I'm seeing all these people who are pretty famous musicians, and then we're working on something that really requires a differ-ent kind of thinking as a drummer. I don't remember Guy spe-cifically saying "play this" or "play that." They hired people to just kind of listen to what the Guy is singing; listen to what he's saying. And I think he gave us a lot of leeway, too. It wasn't like some sessions where you've got people who are just, like, you do this, you do that, you do that. With Guy, it was really kind of free-floating. We just kind of all came together and listened to the song and started playing, If it was heading in the right direc-tion, Neil never stopped this. Guy was happy, and that's how you determine whether it was the way you're supposed to go.

It seems like he had a sort of conflicted relationship with the drums as a concept.

I think that's true. In his ultimate vision, he only wanted him and his guitar. That's it. And that wasn't him being a butthole or anything like that. That's the way his music was. Even though there's three different drummers, and one of the drummers, Larrie London, was a very heavy, heavy hitter. But we all knew what our place was — that this wasn't about the drums. This was about Guy. And so we tempered what we played, and we changed the way we played lots of times just to stay out of his way. That's why, honestly, the stuff that I've heard, you don't hear much drums at all. That's what Guy wanted, and that's what Guy needed. I think if it would have been totally up to him, there probably wouldn't have been any drums on the sessions.

Do you remember anybody specifically hanging out at the sessions?

I remember that there were some young upstarts who went on to be stars, like Steve Earle. I remember the Everly Brothers stopped by. It was almost like a country Phil Spector session, where anybody might come by and jump in and start participating. It was late night, and there was a lot of fun too at the session. I mean, it was serious, but there was a lot of joking around, a lot of having fun.

I think Neil did an excellent job producing Guy. When you have a lot of people dropping by and hanging out or whatever, it can get chaotic, and it's hard to communicate with everybody out in the room. Neil had a great personality for doing that. There was never any tension whatsoever. There was just a calmness on Neil's part to let things happen.

For me, there was a little bit of nervousness, and then there was tremendous excitement, because once again, I'm just starting to build my career. So this is a big deal. I'm working with some of the best players in Nashville at that time who had tremendous resumes. I mean, you've got David Briggs on piano, and you've got Mike Leech (on bass), and Hal Rugg and a bunch of people on steel guitars and fiddles and stuff. These guys were first-call players. There were a lot of things going on in my head at the same time, just trying to do my part and do it well as best I could. So it was a little nerve wracking, but at the end it seemed to turn out well.

STEVE EARLE (backing vocals)

What stands out for you about Old No. 1, fifty years later?

It was the first record I ever got my name on. I'm barely on it. I'm the background vocals, along with several other people, on "Desperados Waiting for a Train." I think that particular track is me, Emmy, Sammi Smith and Rodney. There's no individual credits on the album, but that's what I remember. I think Sammi and I did ours the same night, but not at the same time. We did them all one at a time, and I think Rodney was first.

I wasn't in town yet when the ill-fated first version of *Old No. 1* was made. ... I moved town November '74, and Sunbury Dunbar signed me sometime early in 1975. I was not on any of those (*Old No. 1*) demos the night they were recorded, but I was present when a lot of the overdubs were done. A few of these tracks — I know for a fact "Rita Ballou" — I don't think they knew they were recording it for the record at the time.

Live (in the studio), what went down (on "Rita Ballou") is Guy on acoustic guitar, and the really cool fingerstyle thing is Dick Feller, because he's a great guitar player, and Gary White on electric bass. [Note: White is credited only for harmony vocals on the LP's back cover.] They later added Lea Jane Berinati on piano. And she did play really good piano, but I don't think it needed piano. That was the first time I saw something happen in a recording studio that I didn't agree with. Wasn't the last time. I can remember hearing it without the piano, and I liked it better, because everything focused on Feller's guitar, and Guy played really well against it. It was like Doc and Merle (Watson) — that's what they went for, and it worked. Guy was a folkie, when it came down to it. The first record he made that he liked, I think, was *Dublin Blues*. I think before that, everything was just like struggling, trying to do stuff with the rhythm section, and never really getting the hang of it.

Do you remember how Pat Carter from Sunbury Dunbar got production credit on four songs?

He wanted to be a producer really badly. And "Rita Ballou," he's the producer on it. He was the guy running that session. "Desperados Waiting for a Train," I don't know anything about. I think the song was about two years old, and (the demo) was made when he wrote the song. "L.A. Freeway" I think is the original demo. Maybe they did record a new "L.A. Freeway," I don't know. It gets a little confusing, because *Texas Cookin'* came so quickly behind it, and I was there for nearly all of *Texas Cookin'*. That's when I met Emmy, was on the *Texas Cookin'* sessions.

Do you have a favorite song from Old No. 1?

Just for songs, probably "She Ain't Goin' Nowhere," which I think was his favorite song too, at that point. That's the one I'm the most jealous of. "Desperados" is a great one too. But "Desperados," that stuff for both me and Guy, those long story songs, narrative songs like that, we could do those in our sleep. And so I was always prouder if something was a little more poetic.

But the song that I had the most fun recording (on Earle's 2019 tribute album *Guy*) was "Rita Ballou" probably, simply because I had that same experience that (Guy) did of Garner State Park, like a decade and a half later. So it was something I knew about firsthand. ... That fingerstyle thing that Dick Feller did kind of saved it, because it made it swing a little bit. And my version of it, I'm doing exactly what Dick did, but I'm doing it on an electric guitar. And if you do that, it ends up being essentially that hybrid between honky-tonk and western swing that's pretty much South Texas. You gotta be able to dance to it in South Texas. That's the way country music worked, and that's the country music I was introduced to firsthand.

MICKEY RAPHAEL (harmonica)

How did you come to be involved in Old No. 1?

Well, I knew Guy. I had met him several years prior in Dallas at a little folk club called the Rubaiyat. That's kind of where I learned to play the harmonica, and fell in love with the folkie kind of music that came through there. I don't remember how I met Rodney Crowell, but I was friends with Rodney. So I guess just hanging out with Guy and Rodney and Susanna and Townes — they were doing this record, and Neil Wilburn was producing and engineering. And I guess I just got asked to play on the record, because that was just kind of the group I was hanging with.

The whole Guy thing was really my deep immersion into Nashville. The first time I ever went to Nashville was with Willis Alan Ramsey when he was working on his record, which I ended up not even playing on, but just going for the drive. But then across the hall from that (Ramsey) session was Neil Young doing *Harvest,* and Eric Anderson doing the record *Blue.* So Nashville at that time really held a special place musically for me.

But I was able to be involved with Guy — they used me on the record. I was still kind of a new player. I'd only been playing about five years, and I loved being in the studio more than anywhere. You just have to be spontaneous and be right every time you play. I mean, there's room for mistakes, but every take you want to be a great take.

The impression I've gotten from the other people who I've spoken with who were involved in the album is that there was not a ton of rehearsing going on.

Oh no, there's no rehearsing. And when you're doing studio work, you don't even hear the song beforehand. I had heard some of the songs prior, but any of us who are doing studio work, the first time we hear it is when the red light's on. But there was a certain air of levity. Susanna Clark and Karen Brooks showed up wearing bird suits. I don't know what that was about, but they were wearing bird suits, and sitting around the studio.

What did you anticipate about that record versus what ended up happening?

I never really think about that. I just look at it that it was a great piece of work, and I was really proud of it. What happens to it commercially, if it gets on the radio or any that stuff — we have no control. It's just like throwing darts against a wall or something like that. Sometimes they stick, sometimes they don't. Maybe Guy thought about it, but the musicians don't. I don't think it's on anybody's radar, because we have no control anyway. It can be the greatest record in the world, and it may not get picked up by the radio. ... As much as I love that record, it should have been number one everywhere. But it is a business, it's not about art, in the record company world. But to us it was, and I thought we made a good piece of art. We were all happy with it.

It feels so casual, even compared to other people who were making outside the lines of country music from that era.

Well, you're right, but that's just Guy, and that was Rodney and everybody involved. It wasn't like we were trying to make a hit record. We were just trying to serve the songs. So the recordings were as good as those songs. Neil was a really hands-on producer, and if he didn't like something, or Guy didn't like something, you'd do it over again. So it wasn't just "let's all hold hands and sing kumbayah." There was work involved. It takes work to make a good record. We weren't just phoning it in. I think everybody worked really hard to get the best out of it, to make the best record we could. I was just happy to be a part of it. Because I knew it was going to be great whether I played on it or not, and I wanted to be a part of it.

SHANE KEISTER (piano)

What was your initial impression of Guy?

Oh, I liked him. I remember liking him. He was gruff, but he was also kind, you know? He had such a passion about what he was doing. I really liked him.

Do you remember what you thought about the songs when you first heard them?

As a general rule, I always listen very carefully to lyrics, because lyrics make the song. You know, what we do in black-and-white terms is really just an accompaniment. Can be simple, can be complex, but it's about the lyrics and it's about the song. So I usually let that kind of steer me in the direction that I play. What's he talking about, or what's she saying, you know, and just kind of let it come naturally. Lyrics inspire me. The music inspired me too, not to say it doesn't, but yeah, lyrics get to me.

Do you remember anything about the vibe of the session, or other people you met there?

I think I played on the same tracks that (drummer) Larrie Londin played on, because I remember him in the studio. We worked together a lot. We kind of nodded to each other, yeah, this is gonna be fun, this guy's good — the looks you can give each other.

What was Neil Wilburn like as a producer?

Oh, he was very, very good. He knew not to say anything. The most important part of being a producer is to shut up and let the music happen. As a producer, you guide it, you steer it, but you let it be whatever it's supposed to be. And he was great at that.

STEVE GIBSON (guitar)

Did you play on the demos of some songs that made it onto Old No. 1?

Yeah. Sunbury Dunbar did demos all the time. (Sunbury Dunbar's) Dan Hoffman, whose nickname was DJ Dan, hired me on a few sessions. And that was I think my first introduction to Guy. ... I seem to recollect that a few of those tracks started life as songwriter demos. And were then massaged, or in some cases maybe not massaged, and then converted into master recordings. I don't remember which ones. ... I do remember that doing those demos was what eventually led me to be doing sessions that became *Old No. 1*.

What did you think when you first heard Guy's songs?

My impression of Guy was that, here's this fellow who knows how to write these beautiful words, and the music is so pure, and he's sitting there playing. I remember he gave me a thumb pick that he had made. I may even still have it. He used to take a thumb pick and then rivet a thinner, straight pick down on the bottom part of it, and that way you could thumb-pick, or you could strum with them. He was a good guitar player. He knew how to accompany himself. So I was impressed. Plus I was 19 years old and thinking, boy, these guys are great. And they were great. History has remembered that era well.

Did Guy have much feedback for you on how he wanted the guitar to sound?

I feel like there's a two-pronged answer to that. One is that sometimes, for example, "Let Him Roll" — that guitar part of Guy's is the center of the song. It's a unique guitar part, and as a young musician, I had the instincts enough to say it would be stupid for me to either change this or try to improve on it, or something like that. So a lot of Guy's things presented themselves in a way that a thoughtful person would say, "Well, yeah, maybe I can add something here or something there for color, but it stands just like it is." I don't recall him ever dictating parts. I think that was still an era where writers, and even artists and producers, would assemble groups of people for their talents and what they brought to the table, and then let them loose on whatever the project was.

How do you remember the sessions going?

I'm confident that I recall at least a few of those starting as demo sessions. Everybody was collegial and friendly. ... The magic that happens when you combine half a dozen really talented, brilliant people who are not only good musicians, but they're pretty good psychologists too — when you put them together, everybody kind of figures out what we have to get done here, and then the ideas bounce around. It becomes a collective deal. And I remember that there was the appropriate level of contribution from marijuana. So it was fun. At the end of the day, you would go in and listen to the playbacks. And then you go home and go, boy, I'll fall asleep right away because I want to get up, get to the studio first thing tomorrow and see what's going to happen.

Did the vibe around Guy change a little bit once he once he had the record out?

Songwriters in that era were all rooting for each other. When one succeeds, it floats the whole fleet. I don't remember it changing anything other than giving bragging rights. I could say, hey, I played on Guy Clark's _Old No. 1_. The same way I can do when I say, hey, I played on (Dave Loggins') "Please Come to Boston," which was an enormously big hit record. One was a radio hit and a chart hit, one is kind of an underground favorite. But I'm just as proud of my work on Guy's stuff as I ever was on anything else.

CHAPTER FIVE
THE *OLD NO. 1* TWO-STEP: COMPARING 1974 TO 1975

It's unlikely that the Mike Lipskin-produced version of *Old No. 1* will ever see the light of day, in part because RCA still owns the masters and rights would have to be negotiated. But Guy also made it clear to close friends and peers that he absolutely opposed any of those recordings ever being released. However, in the process of writing *Without Getting Killed or Caught*, Tamara Saviano interviewed Lipskin, who agreed to send her a copy of the recording that he had saved. Saviano has kept that recording tightly under wraps, but because its existence was such an important part of the *Old No. 1* story, she shared it with me while I was writing this book. Toward that end, it seems appropriate to offer some detailed comparison and contrast between the two versions of the album.

When the subject of the Lipskin version came up during the various interviews journalist Natalie Weiner conducted for this book, the comments generally were not favorable. "I remember hearing it," Lea Jane Berinati says. "And when I heard horns on one of those songs, it just — I hate to say it, because I'm a positive person, but actually I'm positive it almost made me sick. Guy's music is so different from anything that's supposedly commercial. I mean, there are commercial songs, and they're great. But to take Guy's music — I know Mike meant well. He intended to do it to benefit Guy. But it was so far from Guy's personality and his music, it just wasn't real. It just wasn't anywhere near, and Guy wouldn't do it. He wouldn't put it out."

Similar comments came from other interview subjects. Pat Carter: "They brought somebody in from New York or somewhere to do an album on Guy, and it was just way, way too slick. Guy didn't like it at all. So they never released that thing." Steve Earle: "That was a pretty dumb move on that guy's part," he said of Lipskin, before adding that "some of it's Guy, and a thing that persisted with him. Guy had a real problem with drums, and it took him a long time to admit that that's what the problem was." Rodney Crowell's recollection is fleeting: "I think Guy started in the fall of '74 recording it. Now maybe there was an early version that got canned." (Rodney's memories may be complicated by the fact that he was hired to produce 1981's *The South Coast of Texas* after a similar situation happened with a nixed early version of that record.)

My overarching impression, after having spent a fair bit of time with Lipskin's version, is that it wasn't so drastically different from the released version as its reputation seems to suggest. I do believe the *Old No. 1* that came out in November 1975 is a better album, but I don't think it would have been a "disaster" if Lipskin's version had come out, as Guy believed. The earlier version had a heavier production hand, yes, but I wouldn't call it "slick" by industry standards, even back then.

Two specific differences with the arrangements stand out. First, the drums. Jerry Kroon's comment in the previous chapter that "you don't hear much drums at all" on the final version of the album is borne out by close listens. That's not so much case with several tracks on Lipskin's version. If Guy harbored issues about drums that took years to resolve, you can see how it would have been a problem for him. Second, the horns. They're not all over Lipskin's version, but they do pop up here and there. Horns are not inherently a bad thing, of course — but they weren't really the right vibe for most of Guy's music, especially on a debut album that would help establish his artistic identity.

Now we'll look in more detail at song-by-song comparisons. Only five tunes appear on both albums: "L.A. Freeway,"

"Desperados Waiting for a Train," "That Old Time Feeling," "Like a Coat From the Cold," and "Let Him Roll." For the sake of clarity, we'll refer to the Lipskin-produced unreleased album as the 1974 version, and the Wilburn-produced album that was released as the 1975 version.

"L.A. FREEWAY"

The biggest overall difference is that the 1975 version feels more deliberately paced. For starters, its instrumental intro is twice as long as the 1974 version; the vocals begin 30 seconds in, rather than 15 seconds on the '74 take. Both recordings begin with acoustic guitar, but the 1974 version adds a touch of keyboards and low-register strings (probably cello), whereas in 1975 the counterpoint to the guitar was an exquisite fiddle run from Johnny Gimble. That fiddle part alone tips the scales in 1975's direction for me.

Gimble's gorgeous fiddle touches duel gently with Mickey Raphael's harmonica playing on the song's extended outro, which runs for nearly a minute and a half. That's almost a minute longer than the outro of the 1974 version. The total run-time of the 1975 version, by the way, is 4:56, longer than the 4:43 cited on the back-cover credits. The 1974 version clocked in at 3:35. Both cuts feature backing vocals in the chorus; those on the 1975 version feel a little more natural, perhaps because so many of Guy's good friends handled the backing vocals on those sessions. Drums are more prominent on the 1974 version, but they're still mostly secondary to the sound and arrangement. The 1974 version also has violin, but not until the final chorus.

Because Jerry Jeff Walker's 1972 recording of "L.A. Freeway" was a minor hit single and thus was how many people (including yours truly) first heard a Guy Clark song, it seems worth briefly comparing Walker's take on the tune. It's more rocked-up than either the Lipskin or Wilburn versions, particularly down the home stretch; backing vocalists vamp through much of the outro, which splits the difference between Guy's two versions by running one minute. I have a sentimental soft-spot for this one because I heard it so many times on the radio in my pre-teen years. It took me awhile to get used to Guy's version on the released *Old No. 1* album; for Guy, it was probably the exact opposite, with Jerry Jeff's version feeling quite different to him.

"DESPERADOS WAITING FOR A TRAIN"

The big difference here is that the primary instrument on the 1974 version is acoustic guitar, whereas the 1975 version is carried mainly by piano. This is slightly surprising, because in general the guitar is more prominent on the later version of the album than the earlier one, which puts comparatively more focus on piano. There's also a difference in tempo: The 1975 version runs 38 seconds longer. Unlike "L.A. Freeway" where the longer run-time for the 1975 take results mostly from a longer intro and outro, in this case Wilburn just presented the song with a slightly slower pace.

Mostly, though, these two versions of "Desperados" are good examples of how a truly great song can be adaptable to many arrangements. I like how the 1974 version sounds with guitar at the center, and Lipskin does a good job of building the sense of tension and drama by adding a little bit more to the arrangement as the song continues: sprinkles of piano, then a flourish of horns, eventually a swell of strings. The 1975 version has a stronger vocal track — especially the key "come on Jack, that sonofabitch is comin'" line — and the more deliberate tempo feels to me like a better fit the song. But overall I'd say both of these recordings are strong tracks.

"THAT OLD TIME FEELING"

The 1975 version has greater appeal for one specific reason: backing vocals. They're not used at all on the 1974 take, but on the '75 version the song's title line gets gradually building vocal support each time it comes around — nine times in all. There's a real warmth and humanity to those accompanying voices that fully sells the spirit of the song. It helps that one of those voices is clearly Emmylou Harris.

The core of the arrangement is the inverse of "Desperados" — mostly keyboard-based in 1974, while fiddle and guitar take center stage in 1975. There aren't many straight-up electric guitar solos on *Old No. 1* in general, but both versions have one in the song's final minute here. The 1975 solo feels more lyrical to me, but it's entirely possible that both were played by the late Reggie Young, who took part in both sessions.

"LIKE A COAT FROM THE COLD"

In what almost feels like flipping the script from the previous song, this time the backing vocals on the 1975 version don't feel as well-suited to the song, which musically is a fairly straightforward love ballad. On "That Old Time Feeling," those vocals feel deeply soulful, but on "Like A Coat From the Cold," they seem kind of forced, almost canned. The 1974 version sounds just fine with only Guy's voice carrying the message.

Both versions are built on an acoustic guitar foundation; the 1974 version accents the picking mostly with strings, while the 1975 take uses keyboards, almost to a piano-ballad type of effect. Of the five songs that both versions of *Old No. 1* have in common, this one's the closest match between the two tracks. They're basically exactly the same length (3:18) and tempo. The 1975 version has no almost no drums; they're more in the mix on the 1974 take, but still unobtrusive.

"LET HIM ROLL"

If the "Coat From the Cold" versions are closest to being the same, the two takes on "Let Him Roll" are probably the most different — primarily because the 1975 version appears to be completely solo acoustic. It's possible there's a second acoustic guitar in the mix behind Guy's picking pattern.

That picking is the base for the 1974 version too, but other things keep getting added to the arrangement as the song rolls on: a light tap on a hi-hat, simple bass thumps, gentle picking on a banjo, atmospheric organ textures, and finally a bed of strings spiked with dobro leads. Everything swells up for an instrumental outro that feels downright countrypolitan.

It's pretty well-done, for all of that — but it's not right for the character of this particular song, which is all about a man overcome by loneliness. The solo approach of the 1975 version captures that spirit just right. It's also no doubt the best example of what Guy really wanted his music to sound like, which gave him an example to follow in the latter part of his recording career.

CHAPTER SIX
RECEPTION AND TESTIMONIALS

Finding the exact release date of *Old No. 1* has proven elusive, but credits on RCA's 1997 compilation *The Essential Guy Clark* specify that it came out in November 1975. Reviews gradually flowed in over the next few weeks and months, into early 1976. In this chapter, we'll quote from a handful of those press clips, plus a couple of entries in record guides that have been published over the ensuing decades. We'll follow that with testimonials from some of Guy's peers about the long-term significance of *Old No. 1*, and of Guy's songwriting in general.

REVIEWS

Ed Ward in *Rolling Stone*, Feb. 26, 1976: "Guy Clark is a red-hot talent at the moment. He wrote 'L.A. Freeway' for Jerry Jeff Walker, Johnny Cash picked up 'Texas 1947' as his latest single, and the astonishing 'Desperados Waiting for a Train' is already an established Western classic. The release of *Old No. 1* proves him an excellent performer too. His voice is not comfortable, but it is extraordinarily expressive and the production showcases it well. 'Texas 1947' is a piece of well-drawn nostalgia, but Clark is as much at home in the present, as in 'Instant Coffee Blues' ... Occasionally, as in 'Let Him Roll,' Clark becomes too sentimental, but generally he maintains the delicate balance that make his songs distinctive. Although listening to these songs one could OD on metaphor and simile, acoustic picking, minimal tunes and sentiment, they represent a healthy direction in American popular music."

Mike Jahn in *Hi Fidelity*, date unknown (likely early 1976):
"It's hard to praise this brilliant album too highly. Guy Clark is a singer/songwriter of immense talent who chooses to work in the margin between country music and traditional folksong. There are others with whom he might be compared: Kris Kristofferson, Jerry Jeff Walker, David Blue, Eric Anderson, and perhaps most of all Ramblin' Jack Elliott. .... Every song on *Old No. 1* is a gem. It's nearly impossible to find a fault in it, so I'll just detail a few spots I especially liked. One of them, of course, is 'Desperados Waiting for the Train,' about a young man who watches his aging mentor grow old and die. 'Let Him Roll,' on much the same subject, is one of the better illustrations of Clark's ability as a writer. He can take a topic that has been oft-used in various forms of literature — in this case the prostitute and the man whose love she rejects — and handle it without employing clichés or getting the slightest bit tacky about it. ... In short, Guy Clark's *Old No. 1* is a landmark recording — the best I've heard this year and one that should be considered quite seriously."

Dale Adamson in *The Houston Chronicle*, Jan. 4, 1976: "*Old No. 1* — the final version, anyway — isn't quite what Clark's longtime Houston fans might expect. The vocals are still loose and lanky, always on the verge of a yodel, but the arrangement of the rest of the music reflects the tight, clean influence of Nashville, where the album was recorded. People like Emmylou Harris, Gary B. White and Sammi Smith dropped by the sessions to soften the rougher edges of Clark's vocals, and the music is sparkling acoustic and steel guitar throughout. The songs — all Clark originals — range in mood from the bouncy, good-timey 'Rita Ballou' and 'Nickel for the Fiddler' to the almost somber 'That Old Time Feeling' and moving love song 'Like a Coat From the Cold.' ... Other songs reveal an equally keen eye and ear for capturing a situation or mood and conveying it in music and poetry. 'Texas 1947' will, eventually, join the classic ranks of train songs like 'Orange Blossom Special,' 'Folsom Prison Blues' and 'City of New Orleans' for its compelling portrayal of the evolution of a distinctly American symbol. 'Desperados Waiting for a Train' and 'Let Him Roll' show an uncanny awareness and empathy for old people that's matched only by The Band's Robbie Robertson, Paul Simon and Randy Newman."

John Tobler in UK publication *ZigZag*, May 1976: "The two particular stand-out tracks are the first and the last on side two. 'Texas 1947' is obviously autobiographical — the story of a six-year-old putting a coin on the railway line, to be flattened by the express train which the whole town comes to watch as it speeds through their station without stopping. And 'Let Him Roll' is a thumbnail sketch of a wino's life and death, and is due for several cover versions, I expect. Guy Clark writes the sort of song that Kristofferson used on his first (and best) album, and that attracted literally dozens of covers. The backing is by Nashville pickers, mostly well known, and especially in tune with this man's songs, and among the harmonising vocalists are Emmylou Harris and Rodney Crowell. Rodney recommended this album while he was here with the Hot Band, and if that should convince a few more to purchase, then fine. Nevertheless, Guy Clark has an exceptional talent, and he has made a record to treasure."

Harvey McGee in *Hank*, February 1976: "On and on through Guy's lyrics, there are pictures and stories of human experience. Songs about a wino in love with a Dallas whore, about a concert in the park, and about his lady Susanna, the one he's chosen 'to walk through this life like a coat from the cold.' ... At this press date, the album is a country pick in *Record World* and even *Playboy* gave it a favorable review."

Playboy, March 1976 (writer unknown): "The ten songs on this album are a catalog of everything worth keeping out of life in the Southwest. 'Texas 1947' tells of 50 or 60 townsfolk gathered at the station to watch the passing of the first diesel train. While they wonder what it's coming to and how it got so far, the six-year-old narrator just grins. 'But me I got a nickel smashed flatter than a dime / By a mad dog runaway red silver streamline train.' Larry McMurtry, set to music. ... The backup has that dry sensibility of an acoustic guitar picker leaning back on a front porch, chewing tobacco, sipping whiskey, swallowing and getting on with the story. It's a treasure."

Greg Linder in *Twin Cities Reader* (date unknown): "Clark's a member of the Kris Kristofferson school of contemporary country songwriters. Losers, winos, trains and busted love affairs populate his melancholy ballads. He writes as well as anyone in the idiom, far better than Kristofferson. As an observer of sad love situations, his eloquence parallels Mickey Newbury's."

Robert Christgau in *Rock Albums of the '70s: A Critical Guide*, published 1981: "I liked Clark's laconic vocal presence at first, although I eventually began to feel that, like the agreeably glopless Nashville production, it flattened this material more than it deserved. Which says good things for the material. A must for would-be Texans and other Western mythos fans. Meaningful sex fans will also dig. B+"

Thom Owens in *All Music Guide to Country*, published 1997: "Boasting an excellent set of original songs — including the contemporary classics "L.A. Freeway," "She Ain't Goin' Nowhere," and "Desperados Waiting for a Train" — and stripped-back, honest arrangements, Guy Clark's debut album *Old No. 1* set the tone for his career. Though he crafted several fine albums after

Old No. 1, he never quite matched its consistency, both in terms of songwriting and performance."

Kit Rachlis in *The New Rolling Stone Record Guide,* published 1983: "Perhaps the best songwriter to come out of the Austin, Texas, progressive country scene. Influenced a great deal by Townes Van Zandt, Clark has a superb sense for the dramatic flourish and the keen detail. There's a modesty to his songs that allows his romantic ballads to balance hard-edged toughness with wry sentimentality, which is more evident on his first album, *Old No. 1,* than on his second and third." (*Old No. 1* rated 4 stars; *Texas Cookin'* and *Guy Clark* rated 2 stars)

TESTIMONIALS
(all interviews by Natalie Weiner except where noted)

Rodney Crowell (backing vocals on *Old No. 1*)
"Guy was the curator of our little early '70s version of Paris in the '20s. ... So basically, I'm still operating under most of the premises that I learned in 1972-73, that particular time. Everything that I learned then about songwriting, I've become more nimble with what I learned, but it is at the core of how I approach what I've done all these years. And in my case, the functional part of writing songs, nobody has influenced me more than Guy Clark. My father would have influenced me in a way that gave me enough of a knowledge of some old songs that I could hang with those guys until I got a few of my own. That's my memory of it. And as far as I'm concerned, I'm still keeping whatever that was alive."

Rosanne Cash (longtime friend to Guy and Susanna)
"It became a thing for me to impress Guy — 'I'm going to make

Guy like something I do, I am going to get Guy's approval.' That was a thing for me when I was a young songwriter. He was a standard, you know. I kind of dissected his songs. Why did they work, the characters in them, the rhyme schemes, everything about it. I worked really hard on 'Seven Year Ache.' I was still living in California when I wrote that, so I met Guy when I was still living in California. And it was pages of lyrics and thoughts that I kind of winnowed down into 'Seven Year Ache.' We were in a dressing room with Guy, I can't remember the show. It was backstage at some festival or something maybe, or a club. I was kind of sitting in a corner, and I just started playing 'Seven Year Ache' to myself. I was too shy to say, 'Guy, listen to this song I wrote.' So I just kind of played it to myself, and his head whipped around and he said, 'What's that?' And I said, 'It's this song I just wrote.' And he kind of nodded. And I was just flooded with happiness and relief.

You know, 'If I can just get off of this L.A. freeway without getting killed or caught' — I lived in L.A. for a long time, so it meant something to me. And also, I love the reference to Skinny Dennis. They were friends with Skinny Dennis. Maybe I only met him once or twice, but I love it when real characters show up in a song.

For me, it was about the great songwriters who were there — Guy, Townes, Mickey Newbury, Kris, Waylon. There were others too, who weren't as well known. And it was mostly men too. It was a standard that I really reached for. I mean, I came up as a songwriter. I was really, really lucky that I had them to look up to. And the kind of ruthlessness — you know, Guy always said, you have to throw out the best line of your song if it doesn't serve the rest of the song. He had a kind of creative ruthlessness that I still adhere to in my mind when I'm writing. Kris did too, and Townes. I just wanted to go that deep. I wanted to be that good. So coming up in that, that was formative. It wasn't so much the records as it was the songs. I mean, *Old No. 1* is a great record, though. 'She Ain't Going Nowhere,' I love that song.

He was definitely the songwriting patriarch of that crew. Rodney looked up to him. Townes did. All of them did — particularly young ones who were just starting like me. He had a Moses-like cast on everything."

Mickey Raphael (harmonica on *Old No. 1*)

"Guy was like Shakespeare or Blake or Mark Twain. His songs were like novels in three minutes. He was just so good at crafting songs in that medium, you know, in getting a whole story or your idea across in such a limited space. He was just good at it. I mean, Rodney was too. I think Rodney was kind of raised on Guy. A lot of great songwriters came out of Texas. But he was just really special, Guy as a songwriter. And Susanna was an amazing artist too. A painter. [She painted the blue denim shirt on the cover of *Old No. 1*.] She did the *Stardust* record for Willie, and *Quarter Moon in a Ten Cent Town* for Emmy. But yeah, he was just one of those guys that a lot of people don't know about, and should.

This record had a kind of slow burn. Obviously, in the moment, it didn't instantly make him rich and famous or anything. ... I don't know what was driving it at that time. I mean, I don't remember exactly who the hot ones were. I know Kristofferson was still in that same ilk, but Kristofferson was a big movie star too. He had a lot of things going. But I think they both kind of came up at the same time. They might have been the same age. Maybe Kris was a few years older than Guy. [Note: About five years.] And Johnny Cash championed both of them. Johnny Cash was a big fan of Guy's. And you see who was cutting his songs — Johnny and Waylon were both big supporters of Guy's."

Margo Price (Nashville singer-songwriter)

"(I first heard *Old No. 1*) in one of my favorite bars ever. It's called the Devil's Backbone, and it's out in the Hill Country in Texas. I was on a tour with my rock & roll band. I was in my early 20s. Of course I had heard Guy Clark songs; I had heard 'L.A. Freeway' before, and loved that song, and 'Desperados.' But I remember being in the Devil's Backbone and I saw *Old No. 1* was in there (on the CD jukebox), and I put on 'Rita Ballou.' And then I became really, really obsessed with that album.

It was a good time to take in Guy's writing. I was getting really serious about writing songs myself at that time. We were on a huge road trip in a Winnebago going across the country. And so when we left Austin and the Hill Country and San Antonio and that whole area, we just blasted *Old No. 1*, headed for Los Angeles my first time ever. I played at the House of Blues, and it ended up being kind of a terrible show. But listening to 'L.A. Freeway' while you're driving to California for the first time, it does something. It shapes you.

I think Guy Clark is the kind of writer you listen to over and over when you're trying to crack the code of what it means not just write a song, but to craft a song. ... The verses go very deep, and then sometimes he had these choruses that were so simple, it was just a repeated line, but there would be so much gravity in that line. I think he just had a way of making songs memorable. I'm still studying his work, just still really in love with what he does. A lot of people will never be able to touch that kind of writing. He was a once in a lifetime artist."

Steve Gibson (guitar on *Old No. 1*)
"That record, I think, will stand the test of time. The music maybe less than the words, because Guy's artistry as a poet, you can't deny that stuff. If you don't get it, you're dead, you know? If you can't see a picture of a runaway streamliner and I got a nickel smashed flatter than the dime — those things have stayed in my mind. Or, 'If I could just get off of this L.A. freeway with-

out getting killed or caught' — boy, I've had that thought a few times. So I think it's going to hold up — as long as people will take the time to find it and be interested in looking at it, and listening to it, and considering it for what its place was in the bigger picture of Nashville music."

Brennen Leigh (Nashville singer-songwriter)

"In *Old No. 1*, there's a lot of South Texas, and there's a lot of the Texas coast and Guy's place of origin, West Texas. So it made me realize that I could write a whole record about North Dakota. He made me feel brave enough to write about where I was from, which I thought no one would care about. So I wrote this whole record about North Dakota. It was definitely influenced by *Old No. 1*. And there was a weirdness to Guy that I think a lot of younger generations than his responded to: You can be yourself, you can write about your people. I don't know of anyone who's done it as well as him."

Lyle Lovett (interview by Peter Blackstock)

"I remember where I bought *Old No. 1*. It was at a record store in a little shopping center in the Klein (Texas) area called Popolo Village. I had a high school buddy who was a year older than I. His name is Bruce Lyon, and he actually was my first partner in performing. He had his driver's license a year before I did, so he could drive us into Houston for a guitar lesson. We'd go in once a week after school. Bruce was more hip to the Texas singer-songwriter scene in those days than I was, so he was forever turning me on to songs that we could learn in our guitar lessons. I found myself really attracted to the kind of songs that sounded complete just playing solo on my guitar, using a finger-style alternating bass.

Old No. 1 was just a natural. I remember buying it on Bruce's recommendation at that little record store. I was interested because of the guitar parts on songs like 'Let Him Roll.' But in listening to the record, putting on the record and listening to it, my first thought was, this isn't just a record. This is a book of short stories. The storytelling, the precision of the writing, the imagery was analogous to what I was reading in lit class, I thought. And listening to Guy's record, it just made me think, wow, songs can be like this? This kind of content can be a song? That was the revelation that I experienced in listening to *Old No. 1*.

As I listened to *Old No. 1*, I'd study the cover, with that painting of his shirt. I'd look at the picture of him and Susanna on the back. And you just kind of place them in the context of every one of those songs. Gosh, you know, 'Instant Coffee Blues' — I mean, they were movies. They were all complete stories and complete worlds within those stories. They weren't simply words and melodies. They were evidence to me that great songs don't need much embellishment. This may sound ironic coming from someone who goes around with a 14-piece band, but great stories need very little support in terms of how they're expressed. And Guy's music was anything but simple, but it was plainly presented in a way that allowed the content to live on its own. Each one of those songs is a whole world that you could stitch together from song to song."

Verlon Thompson (longtime Guy Clark accompanist)
"I went to the academy of master craftsmanship with Guy Clark. I've said this before, but it was like traveling around with Picasso and sitting down and painting with him every day, and sharing his methods and his technique and creativity. I learned so much.

Shortly after I met Guy, I got a contract with Capitol Records to make an album, and I did, and I was not very happy with the whole process. It was something I dreamed of all my life, and I achieved it. And I was empty. I felt like I wasn't being listened to. And I remember kind of whining to Guy about that. And he goes, 'Come go on the road with me, I want to show you something.' He said, 'You don't need bands and buses and managers and all that.' He said, 'What you need is a satchel full of good songs.' I mean, who says satchel? But he said, 'If you've got a satchel full of good songs, you can go anywhere all over the world, and people will show up. And he said, 'You may not be big marquee, you may not be famous, or you may not get rich, but you will have people who come to listen to your songs, if they're good enough.'

My wife walked in last night and we were looking at the *Old No. 1* song titles, and she goes, 'Man, what a satchel full.' I said, 'Yeah, it really was.' So that was the main thing I learned from him, is just to write the best damn songs you can write, and work hard on them, and then go out there and play them with conviction, and play them for the folks. And the rest will take care of itself."

CHAPTER SEVEN
COOKIN' WITH LEFTOVERS

"RCA has a second Guy Clark album due for release in about two weeks," journalist Townsend Miller wrote in the *Austin American-Statesman* on Sept. 2, 1976, as part of a short update on Clark's progress that included a reference to his first taping of the "Austin City Limits" TV show two days prior. Indeed, *Texas Cookin'* came out less than a year after *Old No. 1* — in part because almost half its songs had initially been recorded for the 1974 version of *Old No. 1* that Guy chose not to release. So perhaps this record is ... *Old No. 1.5*?

It was also recorded in much the same way, and with some of the same people. Neil Wilburn returned as producer, once again using some of Guy's songwriting demos as building-blocks for the final takes. Others who returned from the *Old No. 1* sessions included Lea Jane Berinati on electric piano and harmony vocals, David Briggs on keyboards, Mike Leech on bass, Jerry Kroon on drums, Mickey Raphael on harmonica, Johnny Gimble on fiddle, Chip Young on acoustic guitar, Chuck Cochran on piano, and Rodney Crowell and Emmylou Harris on backing vocals. An amusing footnote: Steve Earle sang on *Old No. 1* but is NOT credited on *Texas Cookin'*, though he says he was there for almost all of the sessions. "I didn't play a note," he added. "I rolled joints, is mainly what I did."

Several of those returnees — namely, bassist Leech, drummer Kroon, guitarist Young and pianist Cochran — appear only on "Virginia's Real." The song also includes banjo from Jack Hicks, who contributed dobro to *Old No. 1*. (Leech does have one other credit on *Texas Cookin'*, for string arrangement on

"The Last Gunfighter Ballad.") A note on the LP's back cover states: "This album was recorded in Nashville at Chips Moman's American Studios except for 'Virginia's Real' which was done at RCA Studios," making it clear that "Virginia's Real" was the most obvious rescue from the *Old No. 1* sessions. "Anyhow, I Love You," "It's About Time," and "The Ballad of Laverne and Captain Flint" also were recorded for the shelved version of *Old No. 1*, but the musicians credited on those songs indicate the recordings were fresh takes.

More intriguing are some of the new names added to the mix on *Texas Cookin'*. The title track alone, which kicks off the album, has a veritable namedroppers' chorus of backing vocalists, with Jerry Jeff Walker, Nicolette Larson and Susanna Clark joining *Old No. 1* returnees Harris and Crowell. Studio owner Moman adds electric guitar on the song. Supporting Guy's acoustic guitar work on the track is Brian Ahern, who was married to Harris at the time. Ahern also appears on most of the album's other songs, as do bassist Charlie Bundy and drummer Chris Laird. Guy's RCA labelmate Waylon Jennings turns up on a couple of cuts, adding electric guitar and harmony vocals on "Anyhow I Love You" and also singing on "The Last Gunfighter Ballad." Other notable backing vocalists who appear on a single song include Hoyt Axton ("Good to Love You Lady") and Tracy Nelson ("The Ballad of Laverne and Captain Flint").

Another musician on *Texas Cookin'* was Pete Grant, who's credited with pedal steel guitar on "Good to Love You Lady" and dobro on "Black Haired Boy" (a co-write with Susanna, making it the first Guy Clark song released that he didn't write by himself). Grant had recently moved to Nashville from California. On his website petegrant.com, Grant shared his memories about the June 1976 session:

"My second day in Nashville, Nicolette Larson introduced me to Guy. We sat around that evening in a publishing company office and Guy and Steve Fromholz played songs and I played along on my steel and Nicolette sang. I was captivated, honored, and enchanted. Guy sang some of the songs directly to me, and once, when my attention drifted to what I was playing on the steel, he said, 'You weren't paying attention; you missed that part,' and he repeated the part. He was right, and it was a pivotal part in the song. Our little get-together prompted an invitation to record with Guy the following day.

The session was the traditional, time-tested, approach: Everyone plays at the same time and listens and responds to each other. So, I'm there at the session, as is everyone else: Guy and his band—Danny Rowland, Charlie Bundy, and Chris Laird; and a load of luminaries: Susanna Clark, Emmylou Harris, Rodney Crowell, Jerry Jeff Walker, David Briggs, and Brian Ahern. Neil Wilburn was the producer. So, wow! As soon as I meet these people, I'm playing with them! This is my kind of fun!

Guy walks us through the song, 'Good to Love You Lady,' and I'm pretty sure I get the structure. I get to split the solo with the fiddle. We play it once to get the feel. I'm on my best behavior, in other words: listen intently, play pretty, and don't get in anyone's way. We start playing and I try not to keep reminding myself that, if I mess up my solo, everybody has to start over, and I'd be henceforth remembered as the one who couldn't do his part. No pressure.

So, the song is going along fine. I lay out for the first two verses and come in on the first chorus. The fiddle takes the first half of the solo, and I start my solo based on the phrase he does at 2:01. I come in at 2:06 and by 2:16 I've built my solo up to a point to where it needs a different approach, so I take it into double time and hope I can bring it back to something reasonable in time for the vocal to resume. I manage to bring the last two bars back to the less frantic and I'm done. Whew! At this point, I'm just expecting to fill a couple choruses and we're done. At 3:20, we shuffle a chorus. At 3:46, the end of the shuffle chorus, Guy says, 'One more!' I'm sure we're done, so I start building to the end, getting busier at what I think is the very end of the tune and Guy says, 'Play it!' Yikes, Peter, keep going; do four bars and see if you're to do more. Whew, again! Okay, now I build out. Zany stuff. Good. Done.

The next day, I got to watch some magic by Neil Wilburn, where he got an amazing sound from my very tame and quiet 10-string dobro as we did 'Black Haired Boy,' that Guy and Susanna had written. I had simple little fills in that tune.

Neil had also, amazingly, achieved great separation on 'Good to Love You Lady' with all the vocal and instrument mics. Originally, everyone sang on all the choruses and many sang on verses, and that was the original idea: everyone. But Guy wanted to showcase various voices, a much better idea because of the unique nature of the voices involved. So Neil was able to just pull up each voice as needed. Later on, by the end of the song, everyone is singing. It really builds quite well."

Grant's written account is important, as it provides details of what the *Texas Cookin'* sessions were like from someone who was present only for the second record. Among the dozen or so musicians who appeared on both *Old No. 1* and *Texas Cookin'*, the ones still living sometimes find it difficult to separate their memories of the respective sessions. Case in point: Guy and Susanna's friend Karen Brooks told journalist Natalie Weiner how she and Susanna wore bird suits to an *Old No. 1* session, and that singer-songwriter Carlene Carter (daughter of June Carter Cash) later put on the bird suit. But in a subsequent interview with Weiner, Carter said she'd been present only for the *Texas Cookin'* sessions and not *Old No. 1*. So perhaps that whole bird-suit episode happened during the *Texas Cookin'* sessions.

As for the specific songs on *Texas Cookin'* that were originally recorded for the shelved 1974 version of *Old No. 1*, a few brief comparisons. "Virginia's Real" sounds better to me on *Texas Cookin'*, largely because of the stellar fiddle work of the legendary Johnny Gimble. As for "The Ballad of Laverne and Captain Flint," Guy may not have been fond of the horns producer Mike Lipskin used on the '74 album, but that song has a real swing-like rhythm that lent itself well to the horn accents.

The most notable difference with the other two songs, "Anyhow, I Love You" and "It's About Time," is that each song runs significantly longer on *Texas Cookin'* — a minute and a half for "Anyhow, I Love You" and two minutes for "It's About Time." The slower pace works better on the former tune, and the backing-vocal contribution of Waylon Jennings (alongside Emmylou Harris and Rodney Crowell) provides an extra boost. But dragging "It's About Time" to five minutes feels like too much of a stretch.

Given that "Don't Let the Sunshine Fool Ya" also was recut for *Texas Cookin'* after first being done with Lipskin in 1974, I'd have recommended including that one on the album instead of "It's About Time." But it ended up on the cutting-room floor, held back for another 20-odd years until it appeared as a bonus track on RCA's 1997 compilation *The Essential Guy Clark*. (The credits on that disc incorrectly state that "Sunshine" was on the *Texas Cookin'* album.)

Guy also recalled that "Broken Hearted People," which kicked off side two of *Texas Cookin'*, initially had been in the mix for *Old No. 1*. He told biographer Tamara Saviano in December 2010 that "I had it for *Old No. 1*, and tried to record it. It just came out as a song about drinking, which is something I knew about."

The album's title track was released as a single but ultimately didn't fare any better at radio than "Rita Ballou" had on *Old No. 1*. Steve Earle remembers an interview with Guy from around that time where Guy said that country radio of the era was "a 24-hour-a-day commercial for CB radio." The record label's promotional team "tried a couple of things, but it just didn't catch on," Guy's then-manager Michael Brovsky told Saviano in April 2015. (RCA's Joe Galante recalled that "when we did *Texas Cookin'*, we did this barbecue grill contest where we gave away a bunch of grills.")

Brovsky added, "I can't recall exactly what the political climate was at RCA at that point. That's when people were starting to get involved with crossing country over into the more mainstream pop market. And I think at the end of the day, they weren't certain that that could happen (with Guy), and we went onto Warner Brothers."

CHAPTER EIGHT
JUDGE THE ALBUM BY ITS COVERS

I envisioned this final chapter to be primarily an extensive list including all known covers of the Guy Clark songs that appeared on *Old No. 1*. But first, a word about the actual cover of *Old No. 1*, as it's definitely a significant part of the story of the album.

Somehow Susanna Clark didn't end up as a musical contributor on *Old No. 1*; that changed with *Texas Cookin'*, for which she sang harmony on the title track and co-wrote the song "Black Haired Boy." The visuals, however, are another story. Most of Guy's fans are aware that Susanna painted the image of a blue denim shirt — she titled the painting "The Old Blue Shirt," naturally — that appears on the front cover. Guy provides the in-joke by wearing a blue denim shirt as he stands next to the painting of a blue denim shirt. And that's probably a cigarette dangling out of his mouth, but if it's a joint, it certainly would've fit with musicians' stories of weed flowing freely at the sessions. Guitarist Steve Gibson, who played on the album, had this to say: "To this day, I still think it's the greatest album cover I've ever seen."

The photos on the front and back are credited to the Grease Brothers, the Nashville photo studio that the Clarks' good friend Jim McGuire operated with fellow photographer Bob Miller. The back-cover shot of Guy and Susanna together is telling, as it's unusual for someone who didn't participate in the album's music to appear on its cover. Susanna adds another level of humor by wearing her own blue denim shirt (a slightly lighter shade) in the photo. She and Guy also appear together on the back cover of 1976's *Texas Cookin'*, looking out the back of a truck window.

Those photo placements clearly make a point about the importance of Susanna to Guy's artistry.

And can there be a "cover" of an album cover? Because that's what I'd call the image on the back of Michelle Shocked's 1988 album *Short Sharp Shocked*. On it, the native-Texan singer-songwriter stood with the album's producer, Pete Anderson, for a pose and jacket-design that's clearly meant to mimic the back of *Old No. 1*. I asked Shocked about this in a 1988 interview and she confirmed it was a nod to Guy and Susanna. Michelle and Pete's facial expressions are different, and they're dressed all in black rather than in blue denim shirts, but it's a charming way of paying tribute to the influence of *Old No. 1*.

Let's move on to the list of musical covers, then. In compiling this list, I had a brainstorm about how to spotlight some of the best cuts: A digital "tribute album." This is different from *This One's For Him: A Tribute to Guy Clark*, the 2011 collection co-produced by Shawn Camp and Tamara Saviano, or Steve Earle's 2019 album *Guy*, because those tributes drew from the entirety of Guy's career.

In many respects, this endeavor is more akin to *Frisco Mabel Joy Revisited: For Mickey Newbury*, a tribute album I co-produced with Chris Eckman in 2000. (A fitting connection, given that Guy and Susanna's transportation to their January 1972 wedding was aboard their good friend Newbury's houseboat.) For that disc, we asked contemporary artists to record the songs on Newbury's 1971 album *Frisco Mabel Joy*, and presented them in the same sequence as the original LP. That's what I've done here for *Old No. 1*, except I'm taking advantage of 21st-century technology by assembling already-recorded versions of the songs on a streaming platform. You can hear the results on YouTube at this URL: *youtube.com/@peterblackstock3124/playlists*

A few prefatory notes: After compiling an initial ten tracks, I created a second list of ten different versions. It says a lot

about the lasting influence of *Old No. 1* that two entirely separate tributes can be created from extant recordings. I pointedly
selected ten different artists on the first playlist. The second
playlist includes two names from the first list; it seems fitting
that they are Jerry Jeff Walker and Johnny Cash. I aimed not to
use any tracks from the previously cited tributes, though on the
second playlist I did use one song from *This One's For Him*. (Not
a lot of "Instant Coffee Blues" covers out there to choose from.)

I wouldn't necessarily call these two playlists "the best
Guy Clark covers," in part because the logistics of not repeating artists sometimes meant choosing less-obvious options.
One could easily argue, for example, that Jerry Jeff Walker's
version of "L.A. Freeway" was the most important cover song
of Guy's career; but there's lots of choices for "L.A. Freeway"
covers, and Jerry Jeff was a quality option for other *Old No. 1*
songs he recorded.

That said, one nice thing about streaming platforms is that
if you have a bone to pick with any of the placements on my
playlists, you can quite easily create your own. The long list of
covers that follows these two playlists — no doubt not 100 percent
complete, but it's as exhaustive as I could make it — can serve
as a guide to assembling your own tailor-made *Old No. 1* tribute.

TRIBUTE PLAYLIST #1

1. "Rita Ballou" — Earl Scruggs Revue, from the 1976 album *Volume II*

The North Carolina bluegrass banjo legend teamed with his
sons Randy Scruggs (guitars and lead vocals), Gary Scruggs
(electric bass) and Steve Scruggs (electric piano) on the opening
track from the follow-up to their self-titled 1973 debut. Earl is

the big-name draw, but his banjo — a great fit for the style and spirit of "Rita Ballou" — is just one element in a lively mix that's easy to love. Other musicians on the track are drummer Jody Maphis, guitarist Teddy Irwin, steel guitar great Pete Drake, and pianist Shane Keister. If that last name sounds familiar — indeed, Keister was among the piano players on *Old No. 1*, too.

2. "L.A. Freeway" — Mason Jar Music with Rosanne Cash, from the 2015 album *Decoration Day Vol. 4*

Mason Jar Music is a Brooklyn collective run by guitarist Dan Knobler and his wife Carrie Crowell. If her surname sounds familiar, she is indeed the daughter of Rodney Crowell and Rosanne Cash. So that explains how Rosanne got involved with a fairly obscure indie project. Rosanne certainly had everything necessary for a great "L.A. Freeway" cover — beautifully emotional voice, close ties to the songwriter, and a deep understanding of Guy and Susanna's artistry. The pleasant surprise is that the band — Knobler, drummer Jason Burger, bassist Michael Rinne, mandolinist Jacob Blumberg, vibraphonist Jas Walton, organist Jake Sherman, and harmony vocalists Megan Lui, Hanna Read and Tamsin Wilson — lays down a terrifically low-key backing track that supports Rosanne's vocal perfectly.

3. "She Ain't Goin' Nowhere" — Rodney Crowell, from his 1981 self-titled album

This wasn't the first Guy Clark song Crowell covered on one of his albums, but it was the second, after he'd done "Heartbroke" on 1980's *But What Will the Neighbors Think*. It's a natural for Rodney, who delivers an exquisitely tasteful rendition that benefits from an ace backing cast including guitarist Albert Lee, bassist Emory Gordy and keyboardist Tony Brown. As with Scruggs' "Rita Ballou," there's also a musician who appeared on *Old No. 1*: drummer Larrie Londin. It's worth noting that in addition to recording a Guy song on his own 1981 album, Crowell also produced Guy's 1981 record *The South Coast Of Texas*.

4. "A Nickel for the Fiddler" — Rita Coolidge, from the 1974 album *Fall Into Spring*

More attention has been given the Everly Brothers' version, partly because it was arguably Guy's first cut by a major artist in 1973. But Rita Coolidge's lovely take a year later on her fourth solo album is a better cover, in my opinion. "A Nickel for the Fiddler" was one of two Guy Clark songs she recorded on *Fall Into Spring*; it directly follows "Desperados Waiting for a Train" in the middle of side two.

5. "That Old Time Feeling" — Darrell Scott, from the 2008 album *Modern Hymns*

Renowned as a hit songwriter for country acts such as the Chicks, Patty Loveless and Faith Hill, Scott might even be a better singer than he is a writer. His voice is a drop-dead perfect match for the world-weary poetic elegance of "That Old Time Feeling." Everything's about that gorgeous lead vocal, but there's also tasteful backing from upright bassist Danny Thompson, fiddler Stuart Duncan and accordionist Dirk Powell. *Modern Hymns*, which features a dozen of Scott's favorite cover songs, had been out of print before he issued an expanded edition in 2024, retitled *The New Modern Hymns*.

6. "Texas 1947" — Johnny Cash, from the 1975 album *Look at Them Beans*

Nevermind 1947, here's 1975: It's a pretty good year when you not only release your own debut record, but no less than Johnny Cash leads off an album with one of your songs. "Texas 1947" became a minor hit for Cash, reaching No. 35 on the *Billboard* country singles chart. Johnny's Mount-Rushmore voice is ideal for the mid-century railroad spirit of the tune, which chugs along to a train-song rhythm laid down by the Tennessee Three. And, just like Scruggs' "Rita Ballou," Cash's "Texas 1947" also featured *Old No. 1* contributor Shane Keister on piano. And speaking of *Old No. 1* contributors: guitarist/associate producer

Pat Carter, who headed Guy's publisher Sunbury Dunbar, was the one responsible for getting Cash to cut this song.

7. "Desperados Waiting for a Train" — Slim Pickens, from his 1977 self-titled album

There's so many options for "Desperados," almost certainly Guy's most-covered song. But this was an easy choice, thanks to Guy himself singling out cowboy actor Slim Pickens' spoken-word rendition with extraordinary praise. "He read it as a poem over the music," Guy told journalist Bob Edwards in 2010. "I mean, it was spine-tingling. That's still my favorite version of any song anybody did of mine." The album, released six years before Pickens' death, was the only one he ever made.

8. "Like a Coat From the Cold" — Jerry Jeff Walker, from the 1975 album *Ridin' High*

Certainly Jerry Jeff's pivotal 1972 cover of "L.A. Freeway" is more important to Guy's career. But for the purpose of this playlist, Walker's recording of "Like a Coat From the Cold" fits well. That's partly because not many people have covered this tune — somewhat surprising, given that it's one of the more straightforward love songs Guy ever wrote, and thus potentially it seems to have the kind of universal appeal that often results in more covers. Whatever the case, Jerry Jeff's version captures the song well, with a modest addition of flutes and horns in a few spots that helps enhance the song's melody. Jerry Jeff also tweaked a line near the the start, changing "that old high life is some risky" to "that old high life sure gets risky." I appreciate that Guy was often willing to stick with slightly odd phrases in his lyrics, but I also understand Walker's impulse for a more common-language adjustment.

9. "Instant Coffee Blues" — Jamie Lin Wilson with Jack Ingram, from the 2023 album *Jumping Over Rocks*

As with "Like a Coat From the Cold," there's not a lot of "Instant Coffee Blues" covers to choose from. But Texas singer-songwriter Jamie Lin Wilson gave it a really nice treatment on a self-released album recorded at Austin's fabled Arlyn Studios with producer Scott Davis and guests including guitar great Charlie Sexton. She also called on fellow Texas tunesmith Jack Ingram to sing the second verse, a smart call given that the song is really more a portrait of two people than of one. Cody Angel's pedal steel touches on the song's intro and outro provide an elegant frame to the narrative.

10. "Let Him Roll" — Bobby Bare, from the 1981 album *As Is*
I noted earlier that 1981 brought us both Rodney Crowell's version of "She Ain't Goin' Nowhere" and Crowell's production of Guy's album *The South Coast of Texas*. Rodney was busy that year: He also produced this album for Bobby Bare, who was already two decades and two dozen albums into a fruitful career as a troubadour. Right from the outset Bare makes a change, singing the "Let Him Roll" chorus to begin the song as a sort of preview without giving the narrative details away. He repeats the chorus at the end, in the same spot where Guy placed it. Bare has the right type of voice for the spoken-word verses, and once again there's overlap with *Old No. 1* musicians, as Larrie Londin is on drums. "Let Him Roll" closed side one of *As Is*; side two opened with Guy's "New Cut Road."

TRIBUTE PLAYLIST #2

1. "Rita Ballou" — Vince Gill, from the 1989 album *When I Call Your Name*
It's slightly surprising that "Rita Ballou" is the third-most-covered song from *Old No. 1*, behind the obvious leaders "Desperados" and "L.A. Freeway." ("Rita" edges out "She Ain't Goin' Nowhere" and "That Old Time Feeling.") Maybe that's because it's the most danceable track on the record, and thus

makes for a fun and lively cover. Gill delivers it perfectly, with production by Tony Brown and Emmylou Harris among the harmony singers.

2. "L.A. Freeway" — Band of Heathens with Todd Snider, from the 2022 album *Remote Transmissions Vol. 1*

Like a lot of musicians during the pandemic, Austin-based Americana band the Band of Heathens dealt with the loss of live shows partly by doing weekly livestreams. They welcomed a different special guest each week for an interview and a collaborative cover song. Eventually they had enough for a ten-song album, which included Nashville's Todd Snider joining the band for an admirable version of "L.A. Freeway."

3. "She Ain't Goin' Nowhere" — Nanci Griffith, from the 1997 album *Blue Roses From the Moons*

Though this song works just fine when sung by Guy or other male singer-songwriters, its subject-matter gains extra gravitas with a woman's voice. Like Guy, native Texan Griffith ended up settling in Nashville. She chose "She Ain't Goin' Nowhere" to close her 12th studio album, then went back to Guy's well by putting "Desperados Waiting for a Train" on her next record.

4. "A Nickel for the Fiddler" — Everly Brothers, from the 1973 album *Pass the Chicken & Listen*

In terms of the Everlys' catalogue, this one's a pretty minor player, certainly not up there with "Bye Bye Love" or "All I Have to Do Is Dream." Still, it was a big deal for Guy to get a cut from them, especially so early in his career. I found only one other cover besides the Everlys and Coolidge versions, which made this an easy choice for Playlist #2.

5. "That Old Time Feeling" — Jerry Jeff Walker, from his 1972 self-titled album

"L.A. Freeway" was the game-changing Guy cover on this vital album in Jerry Jeff's catalogue, but "That Old Time Feeling" might even be a better interpretation, its spirit dripping with the world-weariness of that "old gray cat in winter." And yes, that's *Old No. 1* contributor Mickey Raphael on harmonica — so early in his career that the credits spelled his name "Raipheld."

6. "Texas 1947" — Jim Ratts & Runaway Express, from the 2018 album *Small Towns*

Johnny Cash was the obvious choice of this one for Playlist #1, but it's a close call for the runner-up. A more consensus choice probably would be Steve Earle & the Dukes' sparking-hot rendition on his own 2019 tribute album *Guy*. But I was fascinated by how this grassy take from Ratts and his Colorado ensemble shifts to a splendid piano-only outro for the final 45 seconds.

7. "Desperados Waiting for a Train" — Sammi Smith, from the 2022 reissue set *Looks Like Stormy Weather*

If that last track isn't my most controversial call, then choosing this cut over the iconic 1985 Highwaymen version probably is. The way I figure it, these playlists are also a great way to spotlight lesser-known gems. And not many people have heard this haunting take from Sammi Smith, herself a harmony vocalist on *Old No. 1*. Recorded in 1980 but not released at that time, Smith's version finally saw the light of day on a 2022 UK compilation. In fact, the disc ends with a Guy twofer, as Smith follows "Desperados" with "Texas 1947."

8. "Like A Coat From the Cold" — John Clay, from the video series Live at Chicago Music Exchange in 2018

This one's a little bit of a cheat, as I'm not sure Clay has ever released this on a formal record. But there are few available options for this one, and the video of Kentucky troubadour Clay's solo acoustic performance of the tune that appears on YouTube is really, really good.

9. "Instant Coffee Blues" — Suzy Bogguss, from the 2011 album *This One's For Him: A Tribute to Guy Clark*

I've purposely kept tracks from the award-winning 2011 album off this list, so as to not duplicate tracks that already appear on a Guy Clark tribute. But all I could come up with in terms of "Instant Coffee Blues" covers are the Jamie Lin Wilson cut on Playlist #1 and this one. The upside is that Bogguss, with long-time Guy accompanist Verlon Thompson singing and playing along, fully does the song justice. Kind of interesting that the only two existing covers of this one are by women.

10. "Let Him Roll" — Johnny Cash, from the 1987 album *Johnny Cash Is Coming to Town*

Can't go wrong by tapping the Man in Black to close out the proceedings. Johnny copies Bobby Bare's arrangement, adding a chorus at the start to bookend the one Guy put at the end. Cowboy Jack Clement's production is right on target, but as usual, everything hinges on Cash's monumental vocal presence.

MORE COVERS OF OLD NO. 1 SONGS

These are organized by the sequence of the album's tracklist, with covers of each song presented in chronological order. Brief notes are added on a few selections. There are 114 entries on this list; add the 20 on the playlists above, and that's a total of 134 covers of songs from *Old No. 1*.

SIDE ONE

1. "Rita Ballou"
1983: Horseshoe, *Country Boys*
1992: Gary P. Nunn, *Live at Poor David's Pub*
1997: Jack Ingram, *Livin' or Dyin'*
1998: John Denver, *Forever John*
— previously unreleased outtake from a 1980 session
2007: Paul Larson, *It's Just Me & Rita*
2007: Panfil Brothers, *Keep Right*
2009: Toad Hole Flats, *Slightly Out of Focus*
2014: Bill Hearne & Friends, *All That's Real*
2017: Wade Bowen & Randy Rogers, single
2019: Steve Earle & the Dukes, *Guy* (tribute album)
2020: Double-Barrel Music, *Poor Man's Dream*

2. "L.A. Freeway"
1972: Jerry Jeff Walker, self-titled
1975: Spanky & Our Gang, *Change*
— produced by Chip Young, one of the guitarists on *Old No. 1*
1975: Jim Dawson, *Elephants in the Rain*
1979: Plexus, *Life Up the Creek*
1993: Hans Theessink, *Titanic*
1994: Jesse Hunter, *A Man Like Me*
1998: Roger Creager, *Having Fun All Wrong*

2000: Bill & Bonnie Hearne, *Watching Life Through a Windshield*
2005: Gravy, *The Brown Album*
2006: Long Goners, *I-35 Texas Country*
— multi-artist compilation
2006: Beautiful Joe, *Cover Up*
2006: Heartworn, self-titled
— Finnish band
2007: Jimmy Ibbotson, *Canyon*
— member of the Nitty Gritty Dirt Band
2007: Brian Joens, *Foundations*
2008: Flying Shoes, self-titled
— Norwegian band
2009: Two Cat Trailer, *Let's Dance!*
2009: Natalie D-Napoleon, *Here in California* (EP)
2010: Leslie Avril, *I'm Alright Jack*
— Australian artist
2010: Roger Kardinal, *Full Circle*
2011: Radney Foster, *This One's for You: A Tribute to Guy Clark*
2013: John Fleming, *Tones*
2016: Richard Meyer with Mark Babson, *Smoke 'Em*
2017: Phil Dollard, *Somewhere South of the Moon*
2018: My Jerusalem, *Back to the Armadillo*
— multi-artist compilation
2018: Michael Martin Murphey, *Austinology: Alleys of Austin*
— backed by San Antonio group the Last Bandoleros
2019: Steve Earle & the Dukes, *Guy* (tribute album)
2021: Thanatos, *Covered Country*

3. "She Ain't Goin' Nowhere"
1996: Tine Valand, *She's Just Leavin'*
2004: Walking Rain, self-titled
2007: Danny Britt, *Walk This Road*
2011: The Trishas, *This One's for You: A Tribute to Guy Clark*

2012: Catherine Britt, *Always Never Enough*
— duet with Guy Clark
2012: Patrick Brooks, *Rust and Weeds*
2012: Freddie White & Trish Hickey, *Here With You*
2016: Ron Belanger, *Sunday Morning*
2019: Steve Earle & the Dukes, *Guy* (tribute album)
2019: Liquid Sunset, *Covers Vol. 9*

4. "A Nickel for the Fiddler"
2023: Mountain Smoke, *50*

5. "That Old Time Feeling"
1977: David Allan Coe, *Texas Moon*
2011: Rodney Crowell, *This One's For You: A Tribute to Guy Clark*
2017: Kinnie Dye, *Live*
2019: Steve Earle & the Dukes, *Guy* (tribute album)
2020: John McDonald, *On a Magnolia Wind*
2021: Dave Perkins, single
2023: Nick Cody, *Covering These Tracks* (EP)
2023: Brian Hamlin, single

SIDE TWO

1. "Texas 1947"
2007: Andy Owens, *A Melody for You*
2011: Robert Earl Keen, *This One's For You: A Tribute to Guy Clark*
2013: Adam Miller, *When The River Ran Backward: Adventures in Folksong*
2019: Steve Earle & the Dukes, *Guy* (tribute album)
2022: Sammi Smith, *Looks Like Stormy Weather*
— retrospective collection that includes two previously unreleased *Old No. 1* covers

2. "Desperados Waiting for a Train"

1973: Jerry Jeff Walker, *¡Viva Terlingua!*
1974: Rita Coolidge, *Fall Into Spring*
1974: Tom Rush, *Ladies Love Outlaws*
1975: Mallard, self-titled
— includes members of Captain Beefheart's Magic Band and
Frank Zappa's Mothers of Invention
1974: David Allan Coe, *The Mysterious Rhinestone Cowboy*
1977: Texas Lone Star, *Desperados Waiting for a Train*
— Germany-based band; they titled the album for the song
1979: Freddie White, *Live on Tour 1978*
1980: Bobby Bare, *Drunk & Crazy*
1981: Tommy Dell, *Words and Music*
1981: Martin Simpson, *Special Agent*
— English folksinger
1985: The Highwaymen, *Highwayman*
1994: Low Budget Blues Band, *Country File*
1996: Will Barnes, *Texas in My Blood*
1997: Rick Robbins, *Walkin' Down the Line*
1998: Nanci Griffith, *Other Voices Too: A Trip Back to Bountiful*
— multi-artist duet with Guy Clark, Jimmie Dale Gilmore,
Jerry Jeff Walker, Eric Taylor, Rodney Crowell and Steve Earle
1999: G. Thomas, *The Harley Songs Live in Concert*
2005: Hippies & Hillbillies, *Drumless Americana*
2006: Marc Tyson, *One More Try*
2006: Brian Burns, Gary Grammer & Gonzo de Casa,
Luckenbach Compadres
— multi-artist live compilation)
2008: Ray Wylie Hubbard/Joe Ely/Jessi Colter/Walt Wilkins,
The Outlaw Trail Collection
— 5-disc multi-artist compilation)
2008: Pit Baumgartner, *Tales of Trust*
— German artist

2010: Mark Chesnutt, Outlaw
2011: Willie Nelson, *This One's For You: A Tribute to Guy Clark*
2011: Donal Kirk & Friends, single
2013: Tom Courtney, *Guysborough Train*
2015: Robban, *Broken Hearted Again*
2017: Tennessee Jet, *Reata*
2017: JW Roy, Dry Goods & Groceries (EP)
2018: Jerry McGill, *Memphis Rent Party*
— multi-artist compilation; this track recorded in 1974 with producer Jim Dickinson plus Ry Cooder on slide guitar and mandolin, and Alex Chilton on backing vocals
2018: Brenn Hill, *Rocky Mountain Drifter*
2018: Robert Aumann Band, *Love & Memories*
2019: Steve Earle & the Dukes, *Guy* (tribute album)
2019: Jack Ingram, *Ridin' High...Again*
2019: Alex Hardy, *Come Out the West*
2020: Double-Barrel Music, *Poor Man's Dream*
2020: John McDonald, *Even Cowboys Get the Blues*
2020: Scott McQuaig, *As Live As It Gets*
2020: Eric Woodring, *Campfire TX*
2020: J.C. Lens, *The Old Nights*
2020: Rachel Cambrin, single
2021: Steve Varga, *The Good Old Days*
2021: Jeff, *Didn't You Hear*
2021: Mark Mandeville, Raianne Richards & Kyle Swartzwelder, *The Wheel and the Well Vol. 1*
2021: JGroom, single
2022: Gary Maginnis, *Gary-Oke Sessions*
2022: Ramblin Wayn & JP Stingray, *Desperados Blues*

3. "Like a Coat From the Cold"
1982: Chris Rohmann, *Made For Music*
2023: Greg Vajdos, *2002-2003*

4. "Instant Coffee Blues"

No other formally released versions could be found beyond the Jamie Lin Wilson and Suzy Bogguss covers included on the playlists.

5. "Let Him Roll"

2011: John T. Van Zandt, *This One's For You: A Tribute to Guy Clark*
2017: Jeff McDonald, *Life in Glorious Black and White*
2019: Anthony Marks, *The Ramblin' at Midnight Tapes* (EP)
2025: Lost Cowboys, *Lost in America* (EP)